AF472570

# Two Sisters

Arial Green

Order this book online at www.trafford.com
or email orders@trafford.com

Most Trafford titles are also available at major online book retailers.



Printed in the United States of America.

ISBN: 978-1-4669-7600-9 (sc)
ISBN: 978-1-4669-7601-6 (hc)
ISBN: 978-1-4669-7602-3 (e)

Library of Congress Control Number: 2013900474

*Trafford rev. 01/21/2013*

**www.trafford.com**

**North America & international**
toll-free: 1 888 232 4444 (USA & Canada)
phone: 250 383 6864 • fax: 812 355 4082

# Contents

# Dedication

This book was originally began as therapy for myself, I started writing therapy thirteen years ago. I continued to write daily; maybe an hour a day. The therapy was for the death of my sister, Tara.

I would write and shred the pages and begin again. This went on for years, then slowly, I began to write about our entire life and it began to make sense.

This book is dedicated to my sister, Tara, she was an inspiration to each person that knew or had just met her. She could make laughter explode from everyone's lips just by entering a room. She was probably the most caring, loving, and giving person that I have ever known. She lived forty years, and the world suffered a tremendous loss of life and joy the day my sister passed away.

She raised three beautiful children, a daughter and two boys. She raised them to be the best adults that was possible. She also has six grandchildren that adored her. As my sister, she was younger than me, but I looked up to her and admired her greatly. She is sorely missed and always will be.

I also would like to dedicate this book to the many women around the world, that have suffered any abuse, sexual, mental, emotional, or domestic violence. They are not alone and not forgotten by their true loved ones. May God Bless You.

These same women may be depressed; the depression may or may not have been caused by abuse, regardless of the cause, all women hope and pray for the best in all of your lives.

# Prologue

This is personal advice for any man or woman that is planning to read this book. Take it seriously, if I had been given this advice, my life may have been normal. This advice is from personal experiences.

If you are a young mother, remember; your child did not ask to be born. It is a joy and a privilege to be a mother. Babies are a gift from God, they are helpless and totally dependent on you for their care and they need your enduring love and total commitment. Babies should never be spanked for crying, if they cry, there is something they need, and as a mother, you are totally responsible for their needs, without any repercussions. As your child grows, never take anything for granted, all men or women are not created equally. Some men and women have a dark side that is well hidden until the time is right. They can blend in perfectly with their surroundings, but if mother's are cautious, not paranoid, just very good mothering, they may see something that is just not right. It may be a family member, a neighbor next door or a friend across the street. It could be as simple as a touch or a facial expression that makes you have a different feeling, that slight disturbance in your brain may be a warning to watch a little closer. Just pay attention and have a great relationship with your children. They need to know for sure that they can talk to you about anything in the universe. For a child to excel, they desperately have to be assured that they are first in your life, and you will always be there to provide love, safety, and security. If the day ever comes and they realize the love, safety and security is not there, this will cause a tremendous impairment to their self-worth, or self-esteem that will remain with them for the rest of their life.

This paragraph is for the men and women who are so sure they are in love with someone, a person they want to spend the rest of their life with. Please pay attention to their demeanor, their voice tones, facial expressions, these simple observations may save your life or at least prevent an unhappy marriage. Do not let what you think is love color your vision, or disrupt your rational thought processes. Your instincts will usually be right, always trust your natural instincts. Your feelings before a marriage will be the same after marriage, except they will escalate and it will not be in your favor. Do not ever think that you can change a person, because you cannot. The other spouse will always say they will change and they may try for a while; but slowly the change will disappear, and there you are, exactly where you began. The love you once thought was so real will slowly diminish, and you will feel like you are stuck for life and you may be.

Verbal and emotional abuse maybe as detrimental to your mental health as physical abuse. These forms of abuse are present before the marriage vows are repeated, so please pay attention, these men or women are not right for you, run as fast as you can away from these personalities, for your safety and your mental health.

A controlling person will all but destroy you; the isolation is devastating, you will feel like you are nothing. This is his or her plan, to maintain full control. The spouse is aware just how vulnerable you are, he senses your fear, your anxiety, and your lack of boldness to stand your ground. He or she will use these traits that are so deeply instilled within you on a daily basis to maintain full control, and he will succeed!

The loss of a loved one can be one of the most disruptive and sickening episodes that can happen to a person in their life. When two people are so very close, in a very unique manner and one passes this can be a tremendous loss. The loss may cause depression, and it can be severe. This is by far the worst mental episode that any person can cope with. Most people can cope well; they miss their loved one, but they can pick up the pieces of their shattered life and move forward. Then there are some who cannot move forward, they seem to be stuck somewhere in a hole and they can not rise up. Truthfully, they do not want to rise up, they have such a tremendous feeling of guilt because they have remained here on the earth, and their loved one is gone. They are filled with such rage, they hate anything or anyone in their surroundings; in fact they hate the world. These people must get professional help, even if they are positive that it will be useless. The rage and guilt needs to come out, and what better person could there be but a psychiatrist, You may frighten him as you begin to release some of your rage, but they are trained and qualified to listen and read between the lines. They can also learn quite a bit by what you do not say.

A psychiatrist is a doctor; he can prescribe medications that can perform miracles in a very short time. A person should never try to run away from a true depression, it will not loosen its grip, that grip will only become tighter, sometimes to the point of thoughts of suicide. The person with depression needs support from family and friends and as said, professional help. If there is someone in your family that has suffered a great loss and anyone is aware of the person's condition, please encourage them to seek counseling, it may improve their life, or it may save their life.

# Chapter One

## The Beginning

"Arial has not cried for a while, I am going to check on her," said Arial's mother. Eloise, Arial's mother walked toward the crib, not a sound, as she peered over the crib, their first child, a beautiful baby girl lay quietly, not asleep, just lying there, not actually looking at anything in particular, just laying quietly. Arial's mother, Eloise, began to talk to her, she slowly began to move around, she did not cry, at the very young age of about two months, Arial knew not to cry. Eloise checked her diaper, sure enough she was wet and had pooped in her diaper. Eloise changed her diaper, talking to her, Arial began to coo and smile, but she did not cry! Eloise knew she should be hungry, so she prepared a bottle and held her while she emptied the bottle. Arial was hungry, she wiped that bottle out! Eloise talked to her daughter as she fed her, Arial desperately needed this attention. Arial's father, Frank did talk to her some, but only when she needed attention.

Arial's parents, Eloise and Frank, were married almost ten years before Arial was born. The delay of pregnancy was not on purpose, it just did not happen. They always wanted children, and when Eloise finally got pregnant, they were both ecstatic! They were thrilled, married over nine years, trying so hard, finally Eloise was pregnant. When the pregnancy was announced to the family, there was almost a party to celebrate. Eloise and Frank, as well as the families from both sides had almost given up, so when this announcement was made known, everyone was elated. The pregnancy, itself went well, no problems at all. Eloise was so thankful and excited; they had tried for so long, and now she was going to have the child she wanted so desperately. Eloise's health was good and time seemed to fly by, it did not seem like nine months, but the birth was very close.

The baby wanted out, it was time, to the hospital they went, and there was a swarm of relatives gathered with Frank in the father's waiting room. Eloise had been having contractions for several days, not hard, just enough to give Eloise a heads up. This was her first child and she had no knowledge of actual childbirth, so she was not sure about any of the signs, maybe the pain, but nothing more. Eloise, Frank and the family were in for a lengthy labor.

Eloise, before the pregnancy was a small framed woman, she weighed ninety-eight pounds when she and Frank married. The end of the pregnancy came and she looked like a blimp. Of course Eloise was not concerned with her weight or size, she assumed she would lose the weight quickly after she gave birth.

Eloise's pregnancy went well, and she assumed the delivery would be normal also. Unfortunately, this was not the case. Eloise lay in very intense labor for twenty-four hours. The doctor she had chosen did not believe in any extra intervention, she was not allowed any pain medicine and he believed in a completely natural birth. Arial's weight was heavier than normal, she weighed over ten pounds. This little girl simply could not get out of that small area. The labor pains were excruciating for Eloise, so much so the intense contractions ruptured the muscles in Eloise's abdomen.

The doctor was beginning to have concerns for mother and daughter. He went to the labor waiting area to speak to the father. He explained the situation and solemnly said, "I am doing everything possible to save your wife, but I cannot make any assurances concerning the baby." Frank, the husband and father, was outraged, he frightened the doctor. The doctor immediately returned to the labor room, he did not hesitate, he knew something had to be done to intervene. The doctor had always believed in a completely natural birth, but this time he would have to make an exception. The baby was in the birth canal, but being so large, he knew he would have to give assistance. This went against every belief he had ever had, but he knew it had to be done. He decided to use forceps to aid in the delivery, he inserted the forceps around the baby's head and with a gentle pull the baby entered the world. As the doctor was using this method, which he strongly disagreed with, he was not sure of the safety of the baby. This bigger than normal baby surprised everyone, she entered the world screaming, and this sound was a delight to his ears. She was perfectly normal in every way, she had all of her fingers and toes, and she could definitely cry. Eloise, the mother was a definite concern, she was exhausted and in an extreme amount of pain.

The nurses catered to the baby as the doctor's concern was totally on Eloise. The father and family were pacing in the waiting room, when suddenly a nurse appeared carrying a bundle wrapped in a pink blanket, that pink blanket gave it away, the baby was a girl, weighing in at 10 pounds, 2 ounces. The father, Frank was delighted, but where was his wife? The nurse explained that Eloise needed some extra care, but she would be out shortly. There was a sigh of relief from the family, Eloise was going to be alright. Mother and daughter were good.

A few days passed and mother and daughter were allowed to return home. This was a completely new experience for Eloise and Frank. They had been alone for almost ten years, and now there was a third person in the house. This small person named Arial, demanded attention. She had to be changed; to the parents it seemed constant. Arial had to be fed on a regular time schedule, she was a big baby and she was hungry. Arial was upsetting their normal routine of daily life. She was demanding their attention, and if she did not get it instantly she would cry loudly. Frank and Eloise loved this little girl so much, but this little girl had been born with a fantastic pair of lungs. She was really loud when she cried. This little girls' crying was piercing to the ears and to the nerves. One day their last nerve was severed, Frank or Eloise, I am not sure which parent; but one of them picked little Arial up and spanked her little bottom, of course this caused pain, Arial screamed. She was only a couple of months old; this little girl had absolutely no idea why this had happened. This continued each time Arial cried, Arial was being physically abused, but her parents did not understand the word abuse. They honestly thought this was just discipline. There was more than just a few spankings before little Arial's immature brain realized that if she cried she would be spanked. This little girl soon became withdrawn, she lay quietly in her crib.

When Arial's aunts and uncles visited she received all the attention she needed, but when they left, the almost isolation began again. This was so sad for an infant, a child needs attention, love that is given freely, not only when needed. Children need to be talked to and held, the need to be coddled is tremendous, all of the above are essential in the development of a child's brain and growth. When Frank or Eloise changed or fed Arial, they did talk and soothe her, but that was the only time she received any attention. Frank and Eloise were so proud with their accomplishment, they bragged to everyone how well behaved Arial was, even as an infant. In fact, they bragged about this Arial's entire life. What they did not realize was that they had instilled a fear in their daughter that would last a lifetime. All children require discipline, this will almost assure that a child will grow to be responsible, caring, respectful and loving adults. Frank and Eloise used an approach that was so barbaric for an infant. Arial grew, but there was always a fear within her, which later in adolescence and as an adult produced the feelings of no self-worth, or optimism toward life.

Frank and Eloise had five more children, four boys and finally their sixth child was another daughter. Arial was the obedient child, no problems, one might say, Arial was almost a saint. Those four little boys seemed to be quite a challenge for Frank and Eloise. Boys have a tendency to be more active and rebellious than girls, especially when they do not receive equal discipline. The boys grew rapidly, there was fear of their parents, these boys were defiant, and Arial was submissive.

These parents were stern disciplinarians, even with the boys, but it did not seem to accomplish the same results that it did with Arial. The boys were routy, where Arial was quite, she never caused any problems.

Frank, their father was an alcoholic; their mother was mentally and emotionally abused by their father. Frank worked some, when he worked, his income was good for that period in their lives. Eloise worked every day of her life until she retired. Frank was a mean man, not only to his wife and children; but also to perfect strangers walking down the street, it was almost as if he hated the world, he never appeared happy.

Arial never cause any problems, but the boys; well, you know how boys are. They were so close in age, they would fight daily. Arial remembers as a child, Kendall, the oldest of her four brothers must have committed an atrocious act. Their dad was the meanest man on the face of this earth, even with his children. None of the six children would purposely disobey their dad when they were young. Arial remembers one day when Kendall must have did or said something incorrect. Their dad was so outraged at Kendall, he used an electrical cord to discipline Kendall. Arial stood behind a tree, trembling and crying for Kendall. The electrical cord broke the skin and blood began to ooze down Kendall's skinny legs. He was only about nine years old. He was crying so hard, and begging his dad to stop! Arial is much older now, but she has never forgotten this beating Kendall received; she also has no idea why! Arial never disobeyed her parents; this beating Kendall received reinforced what she already knew, do not cross dad!

# Chapter Two

## Tara was Born

Arial's mother knew she was pregnant again, this was the sixth child. Arial's mother decided to keep this pregnancy a secret. She was able to do this because when Arial was born, if you remember all of her stomach muscles ruptured during labor, so her stomach remained large. She continued to work, never informing anyone at work that she was pregnant; she worked until she went into labor. This was a shock to her friends and her employer. Eloise had another daughter, this would be the last child, and the only child their parents spoiled. Tara was her name, six pounds of joy, it took them six children to learn how to be decent parents, at least with Tara. Tara was a happy child as a small little girl. She got everything she wanted, and as she grew she demanded so much more than her siblings. She was a feisty child, the complete opposite of Arial. Tara was determined to do as she pleased, and she received very little discipline, if any.

The time arrived for Tara to start school; well she did not like school even as a first grader. Mother and dad did not have a car, so the children had to walk to school, Arial and her brothers walked with Tara to school, but this did not mean that Tara would remain at school. Tara actually entered the fourth grade, but she hated school. She had no desire to learn, she had other things on her mind. Fun; anything but school, she had friends with the same thoughts. Tara would be taken to school and sent in the front door and she would immediately exit the back door. No one remembers how the school dealt with Tara, her parents had no authority concerning Tara. Tara was determined to do as she pleased. Tara's determination increased with each passing year.

There was one adventure that Tara and a friend did that was very dangerous. They decided they would try to run away from home. It has never been known which one of them thought about this first. They would hitch hike to somewhere; that somewhere landed them in Virginia. That is a long way from South Carolina. They made it to Virginia, and they were surprised when they reached Virginia. They ran out of money fast, considering they really did not have but only a few dollars, which they had stolen from their parents. They also did not have a place to sleep, two children stranded in a city without food or a place to sleep. I guess in the beginning, they assumed they would do great in a new city, oh the wandering thoughts of youth. So young and so innocent, well, maybe not so innocent, very rebellious. They wandered around some city in Virginia, starving, exhausted from lack of sleep, this was not the life of luster they were prepared for. Their young minds thought they could have fun, do as they pleased, with no form of authority. Tara did not like authority, she always thought she was right and everyone else was wrong. This particular adventure was proving her wrong, and she did not want to accept the reality of the situation. It began to sink in to her thick skull that it was not going as planned. They walked around in this strange city, and finally they realized they would have to return home. Their bodies were so tired and they were feeling sick, they were trying to locate a police station. After hours of dragging their feet there it was, a police station! They were honestly happy to see that building, they were not exactly sure how to explain their situation to a policeman. They were frightened, they wanted to go home; not jail! They were lucky; the policeman was very sympathetic, especially since they wanted to return home. They did have enough sense left to provide the correct information, with the correct information the policeman quickly contacted the Kingston Police Department, and both families were notified that their children were safe. Arrangements were made for their safe return; it has been so long ago, memories have faded, no one remembers how they were returned home. I am also sure that Tara was only screamed at, nothing more. She could have gotten away with murder, that is how spoiled she was. Tara did learn a lesson, she never attempted to run away again! She learned that from the terrible ordeal she suffered, not from any punishment she received. Sometimes the best lessons learned in life are from the terrible mistakes and decisions a person chooses.

# Chapter Three

## Tara's Adventures

Arial, the oldest remained subdued; the boys were quite often wild, and of course there was Tara. Tara continued to skip school, she was always somewhere doing something she thought was fun. As an adult, Tara always said there was only one thing she did in her life that she was ashamed of. One particular day, she and a friend skipped school, as usual. They were not searching for trouble, they wanted to walk, they walked and laughed, just two very young girls. They continued their walk until they ended up in a rural area, a field with high grass, a few wild flowers, the sun was bright, then they spotted it, an old building in the distance. They assumed it was abandoned; but they wanted to see what was inside. They began to run, even close to the building it appeared to be abandoned. The doors were locked; curiosity got the best of them, they were determined to get inside! One of them decided to break a window, which one no one knows. One at a time, they climbed through the window; it was dark inside, very dark, considering it was so light outside. Tara stumbled around, feeling her way, she thought that it smelled so clean and fresh. She was feeling for anything, and then she felt what seemed to be furniture. She was rubbing her hand along the top of some type of wooden furniture, slowly her eyes began to adjust to the darkness, as she gazed around the large room, she began to panic; it was a church! Oh my God! She had broken into a church! There were pews, song books, and there was the pulpit! Tara was frightened, she turned and ran to the window, without an explanation to her friend she crawled out the broken window and ran as fast as her skinny legs could carry her. Tara's friend followed, screaming at her; this little girl was frightened also, but she did not know why, she just followed Tara. Tara had always went to church on Sunday's, she was only a child, but she believed in God. The thought that she had broken into a church terrified her, she feared God enough to know that she had done a terrible thing and there would be consequences sooner or later.

Tara seemed to be calmer for a while, but I guess even nightmares fade with time. When Tara reached the age of twelve, she began to see boys, there was a problem, she only saw one. His name was Don, the instant she saw this boy who was five years older than she was; she announced to anyone that would listen, that she was going to marry him. Twelve years old, and she had chosen her husband, well, two years later she did marry him, just as she said.

# Chapter Four

## Arial's Misgivings

Arial was the oldest and first born, and Tara was the youngest and the last child for Eloise and Frank. Arial's short life had been so isolated, she was always frightened but she never was quite sure why. Tara, well even at the age of four she was a burst of energy and mischief. Always was getting into trouble, and there was very little discipline for Tara. There were times Tara would cause trouble for Arial when she was completely innocent. Arial just took the punishment and let it go, she never told on Tara.

Arial's body began to mature by the age of eleven, she started menstruation at the age of ten. She often heard girls talk about the pip; she was never included in these conversations, but she overheard. Pip was the word used for a woman's period each month in the 1960's. Arial had no idea what it meant except there was blood involved. That subject was taboo, Arial's mother as well as other mother's did not care to broach this subject. This was a tender subject and most mother's did not know how to even begin to explain any sexual subjects.

Arial continued to hear the other girls whisper at school and she was curious. One day when she arrived home from school, her mother was hanging clothes out to dry. Arial thought, this was a good time, her mother was alone. She walked across the yard kicking rocks as she stared at the ground. Arial was wondering what words to use when she asked her mother what the pip was. The closer she got, the more flustered she became, then she just asked it," mother, what is the pip?" Eloise always knew this day would arrive, but she did not expect it this soon. She was stunned and quite frankly, she was speechless. Eloise stood there, trying not to make eye contact with her daughter, then she spoke, "you will know when it happens." That was it, Eloise continued to hang clothes, never looking at Arial. Well, Arial was confused, she still did not know what the pip was, end of discussion.

A few months passed and Arial learned what the pip was. At first it was only pink, but as the months progressed it darkened. Arial was mystified, she threw her panties in the trash, soon she had very few panties. Eloise soon realized that Arial had started her period. Arial felt guilty, her mother worked every day, but her dad was usually gone. Arial knew her mother would have to buy more panties and those horrible pads, Arial also knew her mother had very little money, this was another burden on her mother.

Arial's dad worked very little, when he worked and did not drink, things were good, but that never lasted too long. Arial's dad would just leave, without any reason, Frank always left when Eloise was at work. He would get dressed in a nice suit, Frank always wore the best suits, he purchased his suits from the only men's shop in town, and they were first quality suits. Eloise and their six children did not have this luxury, they only had the clothes they needed, cheap clothes.

Frank would dress in his fine suit; he always had money in his wallet, not just a few dollars, but hundreds. He would call a taxi, and leave for Chanston, a large city about fifty miles away. Frank always went to the worst section of the city, an area that was frequented with prostitutes and beer joints. He would pile up in a flea bitten hotel and he had unlimited use of prostitutes. The prostitutes would steal his money, glasses, and sometimes his suit jacket. Two weeks would usually pass, and then Frank would call Eloise, he was in jail, he needed money for bail; and of course Eloise always came to his rescue. Eloise never had four or five hundred dollars so she had to borrow the money from a loan company. Eloise dreaded having to borrow the money, this was a regular occurrence. She always had loans to pay off, and it was always because of Frank and his spiteful adventures, she did not drive, so she walked to town, borrowed the money and then she walked back home. She was always exhausted, she worked every day, raised six children, basically on her own; then she catered to Frank.

Eloise would arrive home with the money, and for some strange reason, she would instruct Arial to return to town; to the Western Pacific, to wire the money to Frank. Arial never understood this, but she always did as she was told. Later in Arial's life, as an adult, she wondered about certain things, if her dad was in jail, how did he get the money from the Western Pacific? Arial began to put the pieces together, her dad had scammed her mother their entire life. Arial finally realized that her dad was not in jail, he wanted more money. He knew for sure that Eloise would believe every word he spoke. It was always another week before their dad returned home. The children did not want him to return home, he would definitely be drunk, and they were frightened of him. The slightest hint that dad was on his way home, the children would scatter in all directions. They knew his demeanor would be atrocious. They each hated to leave their mother alone to deal with their dad, the drunk, but they assumed their mother could handle the situation, she always had. These children all under the age of twelve, were frightened of their dad when he was sober, but when he was drunk, the home environment was much worse.

# Chapter Five

## Arial's Adolescence

Arial's body had reached adolescence; she was tall for her age, skinny, but her body was beginning to develop into a young teenager's body. Small breasts became visible, Arial was so self-conscious, she walked with slumped shoulders, hoping to hide them, she did not want to be noticed.

Arial was noticed, she was a pretty girl, tall for her age, beautiful curly hair, and she appeared to be older than twelve years old. She was very shy and usually alone. Frank and Eloise worked, well Eloise did, and Frank worked sometimes. Arial was the oldest, she had to clean house each day and help care for her siblings. Thankfully, her grandmother lived across the street, so she did have help caring for her brothers and sister, Arial mostly had to do all the housework. This was a lot of work for a twelve year old, she had to have everything completed when her mother arrived home from work. There was no time allowed for fun, this was Arial's daily routine; she assumed this was normal. She knew they were poor, she often wondered how the rich kids lived. Arial knew that some of the kids at school had lots of money, she could tell by the way they dressed. She was quite at school, no friends; she was very anti-social, not by choice, she simply did not know how to communicate with others. She was so shy, and very alone.

Arial was being noticed, but it was not by her peers, it was by a relative, Frank, her father. When Frank was home, Arial noticed her dad staring at her, and it was a stare that made Arial very uncomfortable. It was something about his eyes, and a slight grin that made Arial want to run. She tried to believe it was only her imagination, but imagination or not, she did not like those stares. She was bewildered and slightly frightened. This was her dad, why was he staring at her in such a manner?

Arial tried to stay at her grandmother's house as much as possible, but she had to do the housework even if her dad was at home, he certainly would not clean anything. She did not reveal to anyone the stares she was seeing from her dad, she was not sure what the stares meant, she began to watch more carefully. Arial cleaned the house as quick as she could, she did not want to be in the same room with her dad. She tried to watch him as closely as possible, and he always had that creepy look and that slight grin, barely noticeable, but Arial saw it. There was a feeling of fear that instantly hastened the housework, Arial wanted to run from the house to her grandmother's. She would be so glad when her mother returned from work!

Arial was so happy to see her mother walking up the street. Arial felt sorry for her mother, she walked slow, she appeared to be so tired, she was slightly heavy and this caused her to be even more tired. Sometimes Arial thought that her mother dreaded coming home, she had six children to deal with and a worthless husband. Eloise would rest at bedtime, she did everything Frank asked her to do, she had to cook supper, the children had to have bathes, but Arial helped her with the dishes. Eloise loved her husband, but she really did not like him, maybe she was scared, she tried to silence the boys, their constant antics seemed to get on their dad's nerves. Eloise knew the consequences of upsetting her husband. The boys would receive a belt across their behinds if they walked in front of the television when the news was on. They knew this, but boys will be boys. There was one problem; their mother never intervened with any discipline their dad dished out, regardless of how severe the punishment was, and sometimes it was very severe. Their mother never said a word, she went to another room. The children knew that their mother was frightened of their dad, but she still loved him. As adults the children could never remember their dad hitting their mother, but they remembered the verbal and emotional abuse their mother received. Eloise just accepted the life she had and suffered silently.

Eloise always knew where Frank was going when he left for one of his adventures, she knew he would be drunk and with a whore, probably more than one, but she always allowed him to return home.

Arial continued to keep her fears concerning her dad a secret, but she was very careful even when her mother was present. She wondered if no one else was aware of these stares, were they blind? The house could be filled with people, but Arial was very aware of the stares, but no one else seemed to notice them. Maybe it was nothing, but Arial could not shake the fear and confusion.

Arial's dad's actions began to shift, if they passed each other, he would slightly brush against her, slightly, but it only increased Arial's fear and uncertainness. Arial took every precaution, she would cross the room in another direction to avoid her dad. This was so sad for Arial, she loved her dad, maybe not the heartfelt way that most daughter's loved their dad, but she did love him. She did know that she should not be afraid to be in the same room with him, this was not normal. Arial was thirteen years old, she knew a little about sex, but her knowledge consisted of only rumors she heard at school.

One summer morning, Arial overslept, her mother was working, and the boys were playing outside, and Arial was soundly sleeping. She normally locked her bedroom door when she went to bed at night, but somehow it was not locked that morning. It was probably mid-morning, Arial was sound asleep, laying on her stomach, she did not hear anything. She did feel movement, but she was really asleep, she slightly moved, but only slightly. Then she felt more movement, this time it interrupted her sleep enough that she opened her eyes. She did not see anything, she was still very groggy, but she knew she felt the bed move. She raised her head from the pillow, she also wondered if she had been dreaming; she raised herself up and looked toward the back side of the bed. Oh my God, it was her dad; he was trying to get in the bed with her! Arial was scared out of her mind, she threw the sheet from her and jumped from the bed and ran as fast as she could. She ran out the front door and up the street to her grandmother's. Arial's grandmother knew something was terribly wrong, but Arial refused to answer her questions. Her grandmother was a very wise lady, she also had great instincts. She could see the fear in Arial's eyes, the mounting anxiety, Arial was in a panic! Arial was so afraid her dad would come for her, and she was determined not to go back home. She felt safe with her grandmother. Arial and her grandmother pulled the drapes away from the window, there was a clear view of the road; there it was, a taxi drove to Arial's house, only a few moments passed and Arial's dad was scurrying to get to the taxi as fast as he could. Frank knew he had to get away, he knew what he had tried to accomplish was not appropriate. Somehow, he had managed to dress in his best suit, God forbid that he would depart for his usual adventure without being dressed. The taxi pulled off and out of view. Arial could feel the fear and dread slowly drain from her body. He was gone for now, but he would surely return in a few weeks.

Eloise returned from work at her usual time, Arial did not mention a word to her mother, concerning the episode with her dad; Eloise was told that Frank had left in a taxi. Eloise just shook her head with disgust, and continued with her day. She knew where he was going, it hurt her feelings, and she was so mad, but she managed to hold it together. Frank had always made Eloise feel as if she was nothing, and every time he ran off her self-worth was lowered to a deeper degree. She knew where he was headed and she was well aware of the things he would do when he got there. This was so sad for Eloise, she really loved this man, and the hurt and pain went so deep.

The children did not care if he ever returned home; life was pleasant when he was gone. They were not frightened to be at home, but they understood that he would return. Arial and her brothers and sister enjoyed this time, they could laugh and play without fear of a beating. Eloise was a stern disciplinarian, but never to the degree that Frank was.

Frank would call after about two weeks, he was in jail for public drunkenness, he needed money for bail; he knew that Eloise would wire him the money, she never failed him.

# Chapter Six

## Tara's Fears

Time passed slowly for these six children, faster if their dad was gone. Arial was in high school, the boys were in junior high and Tara, well she had one thing on her mind; Don, the boy she said she would marry. If there was any way possible Tara would skip school, Don was out of school, and Tara meant to see him, regardless of how many times her parents had forbid it.

Tara had quite a bit of stress in her life for a twelve year old. She had to deal with her dad just as Arial had. Tara did not know about Arial, and Arial did not know about Tara. This was a well-kept secret; the sisters were not close at this time in their life, in fact Arial really almost hated Tara. There was seven years difference in their ages, Arial thought she was grown, and Tara was a thorn in her side. Their mother made Arial take Tara everywhere she went. They also had to share a bedroom, this Arial hated. Tara was not thrilled about the arrangement either. When bedtime came; Tara knew to stay on her side of the bed. If she touched Arial even by accident, Arial would punch her. Poor Tara, she had to hang on to remain in the bed. Arial did not care, she could not stand to be touched in the bed. Arial was very quiet and she was a push-over, but there were a few things that would light her fuse, and touching her was one of them.

Arial had absolutely no inclination that her dad was trying to mess with Tara. She looks back now and wishes that Tara and she had been closer. They could have stood together, it was Arial's fault that they were not closer. Arial is older now, and if she had only known, she would have tried to help her sister. They say hind-sight is 20/20, too late to go back and correct mistakes, but one should ponder on the mistakes made and try to never allow the same mistakes to occur twice.

Tara was a very tiny framed girl, and short in stature, but she was very feisty. She was the exact opposite of Arial. Tara would try anything once, but Arial, she did not have the guts or backbone to try anything other than the normal. She seemed to always be in the shadows, alone with an insecure facial expression, everyone could see this, but they chose to ignore it. Tara would not be ignored; she was determined to have fun, at any cost. She did not care what people said about her, words she said would not harm her.

Dad was her only fear, her small body had matured slightly, she was so tiny; maybe a size one. She also had noticed the funny stares from her dad, but she chose not to inform anyone. She also stayed at her grandmother's almost every night. Those same uncomfortable feelings Arial had, Tara also had. Tara, even with her spunkiness, was frightened. There were always small innuendo's that concerned Tara, weird stares, slight touching that forced Tara to watch her dad closely. As with Arial, the same applied to Tara, but neither was aware of the other.

One warm summer morning, Tara and her brothers wanted to go to the city park. Their mother was working, and their dad was home. Tara's brother's asked their dad if they could go, he stood there shifting his eyes from his son's to his daughter, each of them wanted to go really bad, but none as desperate as Tara. She definitely did not want to be left behind, but somehow inside she knew dad would not allow her to go. She was correct, he immediately said the boys could go; but Tara had chores to do, she could not go. Tara knew exactly what was going to happen, and she was frightened. Tara's dad was a big middle-aged man and Tara was so small. Tara's dad began to roll out the orders. There were many chores he wanted her to do but the first one was to clean his bedroom, the anxiety began to build, she turned and went in the house, he was somewhere behind her, she knew she had to be aware at all times where he was. She was smart to be so young, she listened for his footsteps, or any sound that would alert her as to his presence. She proceeded straight to his bedroom, she had to be quicker than her dad. She heard his steps as they slowly approached the room, she did not look back, she knew he was there. She began by straightening the sheets on the bed, she heard the door creak, he was inside the bedroom. Tara could feel her heart pounding from fear, she had to do this right or she would never make it outside. There was a second door in the room leading to another bedroom, she had to get to that side of the room. He was watching her, thinking this was it, he had her, and there was no way she could escape! Frank did not realize how smart and witty his youngest daughter was. Tara understood that she had to be at least ten steps ahead of her dad, silently, Tara realized that this day would arrive; she thought she was prepared, but things occur at the most unpredictable times. Tara quickly moved to the end of the bed to tuck in the sheets, she was observing him, in a very discreet manner, she desperately needed to reach the other side of the bed. Her dad had not even moved, he watched continuously, waiting for what he thought was the best time to pounce. Tara was well ahead of him, she finally was on the other side of the bed. She continued to straighten the sheets, her small body could barely reach the middle of the bed, as she stretched across the bed, oh she was watching him. Frank was not prepared, his thoughts were interrupted by the arousal he was feeling as he watched his youngest daughter. Suddenly with no apparent warning, he grabbed Tara as she stretched across the bed, he had a tight grip on Tara's wrists. He was trying to pull Tara onto the bed, but he underestimated Tara's strength, she began to scream and Frank slowly lost his grip. Tara had been fighting so hard she fell to the floor, this was good; the door was at her feet. Her dad was lying across the bed, stunned, he had been completely caught off guard. Tara crawled through the door and stood up, she looked back, there that crappy excuse of a dad still lay across the bed. Tara took off, she ran the complete distance to the park, she had to find her brothers, she cried, but she was also very furious. Quickly she located her brothers, when they saw her running, they were certain something was amiss. They were not expecting what she had to say! Tara began to explain, it was hard, and she was out of breathe, but they could hear parts clearly; they knew what had transpired. Kendall, the oldest brother was madder than hell; he started running as fast as possible. He was going to kill that son of a bitch! It did not matter how fast Kendall ran, it would not be fast enough! When he arrived home, his dad was gone. Kendall was in a rage, he would have killed his dad if he had arrived sooner. It was good for Kendall that his dad was gone, Kendall could have ended in jail!

Their mother finally arrived home from work, this time she was informed of everything that had taken place. She felt sorry for her children, but she did not have a clue as to how to deal with the situation. This also was swept under the rug, it was never mentioned again.

Arial was never told about these events concerning her sister, it was years later in her adult life when she discovered it, and it was an accident when she was told. She was shocked, years had passed, Arial and Tara were married and had children of their own.

Arial's last encounter with her dad was when she was in the eleventh grade. Arial had never participated in any type of sports in school, but she finally decided to try out for track. This was a major accomplishment for Arial, and this did mean less time at home. Arial was tall and slim with well-defined legs, not only did she run track, but she decided to try jumping hurdles too. She excelled in both ventures. One morning she was jumping hurdles, it was a breeze for Arial, well, it had been until that day. She loved to run, she loved the sun shining on her face, and the feeling of the air blowing through that head of curly hair. She was fast and could easily clear the hurdles. Something went awry that morning, maybe her timing was off, she was near the end and she was tired, who knows. She was running toward the next to last hurdle, her right leg cleared but the left one tipped the hurdle. In one instant she was on the asphalt, the pain was almost unbearable. Blood was oozing down her leg; it appeared the fall had removed the top layer of skin. This was from her knee downward. The school nurse immediately began cleaning her leg and applying antiseptic. The nurse wrapped it with gauze and they assumed she could continue with the school day. Arial went to her next class, hobbling slowly, it hurt to walk. Her leg was throbbing; sitting in a class for forty-five minutes caused the wound to stiffen. Each time she changed classes there were stairs to climb. When she tried to walk, the wound would begin oozing blood again. Regretfully, she asked to go home early. She had to walk home, which was about four miles, this was torture. Arial thought as she walked, maybe she should have remained at school, too late now, she was almost home.

Somewhere during this painful walk she remembered that her dad was home and she was almost positive her mother was working. Arial thought, what had she done? Frank, her dad would be there and no one else. The nervousness began to creep through her, she was almost at the street she lived on, she dreaded to make that turn. Arial could feel her heart pounding in her chest; she had a clear view of the house from the end of the street. She did not see anyone on the porch, which did not insinuate anything. Good Lord, he could be anywhere. Arial took deep breathes hoping to calm herself down, she was not succeeding too well. She had to continue to walk, but she was purposely walking slower. It really did not matter how slow she walked, she would arrive home sooner or later, and she was just about there. She approached the house with caution, peering toward the side and the backyard; no one. There she was, directly in front of the hose, she strained her eyes; hoping to see through the picture window, but there was a glare on the window panes. She was not close enough, the front door was open, that was not good. She proceeded to the walkway, sneaking a peek in every direction. Arial stepped onto the front porch, what was she going to do? She needed desperately to know where her dad was, she moved closer to the window, from this location she could see into the living room. He was not in the living room, dang it; where was he? Arial's only option was to enter the house and hope for the best. She tried to open the storm door quietly, but that metal handle sounded in her ears like a hammer hitting the handle. She closed her eyes and took another deep breathe, she was very frightened. A child should never feel this amount of fear when entering their own house, but Arial's life had always existed filled with fear. The door closed behind her, so loud; she jumped! She jumped once more; she heard movement in the kitchen.

There he was, his head protruding just enough; then he moved forward, standing in full view smiling. Immediately he saw the bandages on her leg, of course he inquired as to what had happened. Was he truly concerned or was this an act? Arial explained the hurdle mishap, and he wanted to see the wound. Oh dear Lord, was this genuine concern, it appeared to be, his facial expression seemed to show that he really cared. Arial proceeded to unwrap the gauze, the skin continued to ooze blood; it looked like a piece of raw meat. His opinion was that it needed to be cleaned again, and an antiseptic reapplied. Arial explained that the school nurse had treated her leg earlier, but he insisted. He left the room to get the cotton balls and the antiseptic, Arial sat in the chair waiting and dreading his return. Please God, let this be a true caring moment, Arial thought, just help me get through this and let him be a real dad.

She was deep in thought, hoping and praying for the best, so much so she did not hear him reenter the room, she was so startled when she realized he was back! There he stood, staring at her leg. Arial had her leg propped on a chair, her dad proceeded to open the antiseptic, Arial was wondering; was he really going to be a true dad? There was his hand, approaching her leg, he started at the top of the wound, but instead of proceeding downward, instantly his hand raced completely up her thigh! Arial screamed, and jumped up, her dad was a large man compared to Arial; but she pushed him backwards. Arial then reached for a dining room chair, with all her strength she threw the chair at her dad. She was not sure if she hit him because she was running as she threw the chair. She ran from the house to her grandmother's house, this was their safe haven. This time Arial told everything, her grandmother tried to console her as she cursed Arial's dad. Arial was crying, and jerking from fear! She began to explain, for just a few moments she honestly thought that her dad was going to do the right thing. Of course, this did not happen; exactly the opposite, exactly what Arial feared the most. She remained with her grandmother, together they stared from the window, and both were expecting his departure, there it was, a taxi arrived in front of the house. Only a few moments passed, and Arial's dad walked hastily to the taxi, then he was gone. Relief, seemed to extend through Arial's body, as well as her grandmother's.

Arial knew she would definitely inform her mother, and that would include the past and present episodes. Arial was so stressed and so tired of the fear, she just knew her mother would handle everything. Arial would be deeply disappointed and hurt, but at this moment she was not aware of this. There was never any doubt in Arial's mind that her mother would be alarmed. She waited with her grandmother until her mother returned from work, then she went home. There was her mother, never expecting to hear what Arial was going to reveal to her. Arial's mother was so tired and this would only add another burden to the mountain size of burdens she had to face each day, but this time it had to be told.

The first thing Arial's mother asked was, "where is your dad?" Arial's first response was that he had left in a taxi. Eloise, Arial's mother just shook her head. Arial knew she had to reveal everything to her mother, for her own safety. She allowed her mother time to pour a cup of coffee, sit down and rest for a few moments before she began. Arial slowly began from the present and went backwards, she informed her of the stares. and the small purposely touching that her dad had been doing for years. Arial also disclosed to her mother the episode when her dad managed to get into the bed with her. Her mother just sat there, with no response, there was an occasional shake of her head, nothing more. Arial was in disbelief, she expected so much more from her mother! Arial was her oldest daughter, did she not believe her? Arial knew how much her mother loved her dad, but Arial was her child; did she love her husband more than she loved her children. Arial realized that day that she should never expect any safety or a feeling of security from her mother. This realization hurt Arial so extremely, the tears flowed freely down her face, the distraught Eloise saw in her daughters face did not receive a response either. This incident was also swept under the rug, as always.

A couple of weeks passed, Arial was sitting alone in the living room, and her mother was in the kitchen. The phone rang, Eloise answered the phone, and low and behold it was Arial's dear old dad. Arial was within hearing distance, but she only heard her mother's words, Eloise said, "why did you try to do that to her?" Arial never knew what her dad's response was, but it did not matter, that was the last time her mother ever mentioned the subject. Of course, Arial's dad needed money to return home, and of course Eloise had Arial wire it to him. Arial was astonished to realize that her mother would allow her dad to return home after he had attempted to rape his own daughter. She did allow it and maybe a week later; there he was, drunk as a skunk. All six kids seemed to vanish into thin air, they had no intention of remaining at home when he was sober, much less when he was drunk. Arial's dad had been home for about a week, he was sitting in the kitchen, Arial needed something crucial from the kitchen, so she defiantly marched passed him, he spoke, and Arial paused, he said, "your mother told me that you said that I tried to rape you," Arial's reply was, "you did try to rape me!" Her dad replied, "I have needs too," Arial eyes pierced at him with hate, she said, "not with your daughter!". Arial turned and walked out the front door, she was so mad, who did he think he was? The years passed and other victims began to surface, he had tried unsuccessfully to rape several nieces and his granddaughter. Everyone kept their secrets hidden until they got older. They all assumed that like Arial and Tara that no one would believe them, but they were all frightened enough to stay away from him.

Every child, and there are many, that are sexually abused or there has been an attempt of sexual abuse should always tell someone as soon as possible. It is not the child's fault, they are usually frightened into thinking something bad will happen to them or their family. If Arial and Tara had been closer during this time in their lives, maybe they would have confided to each other. It took Arial until she was in high school to confide in anyone, and it was her grandmother. Tara told at a much younger age, but it was told to her brother's initially, then her mother.

There are guidance counselors at school, most are very understanding, and sessions are confidential. It does not matter who, just inform someone, a priest, counselor, friend, there will be someone that will believe you.

There can and will be devastating consequences that can affect you as a person throughout your entire life. You may not be aware that those secrets are causing so many problems in your life. So please, tell; do not keep it buried inside yourself, it can destroy you as a person.

# Chapter Seven

## Arial and Clark Before and After Marriage

Arial was seventeen years old but she had only had two dates in her life, that may have been a good thing, she was so submissive, quiet and she always did as she was instructed. Then Clark entered her life, he was not new to her, they had grown up within a block of each other. He was five years older than Arial and was in the Army the first time he asked her for a date. Arial was only sixteen years old and had never actually been asked for a date. She knew he was older and she was weary of him, Arial was weary of all boys or men. She had a very troubled childhood and she was so insecure. She was not street smart like Tara. Arial's entire life had been so isolated, she could not seem to start a conversation with anyone. She did not have any knowledge of how to talk to Clark. He was persistent, he would not give up, and he would stop his car on the street probably every other day and ask her out. Finally after numerous attempts, Arial agreed, she really did not want to go but she was going. Oh Lord, when he arrived she was a nervous wreck. Arial was dressed casually, skirt and blouse; Clark was, well lets just say he went over-board with his attire. He was dressed in a suit with a bow tie, a bow tie!!! Arial knew no one that dressed in that manner. This was terrible, Arial was almost embarrassed to be seen with him, and she was laughing to herself. This was not Arial's normal demeanor, she usually accepted life as it occurred. This was just too much, if Clark had only known what Arial was thinking, he would have been terribly embarrassed. Arial was determined to do the right thing and not be rude, she prayed they would not encounter anyone she knew, she would be mortified. Arial was only sixteen years old and she did not have or want the same dress code as Clark.

There were not a lot of activities or places for two people to be entertained in Kingston. The movies or hamburger joints to eat at, so Clark made the selection; a drive-in movie. The first thing Arial saw as they drove toward the entrance was the name of the movies, NINE SIN-SATIONAL MOVIES, she did not approve of the name, but she thought she would give it a chance. This was a mistake, the first scene was a woman dressed in only an apron, nothing more. The woman's breast were bouncing around with very sexual overtones. Arial did not complain, but she was not viewing the screen. Clark noticed Arial's disinterest in the movie, but decided to prolong this as long as possible, hoping Arial would begin to show interest, but this did not happen. Clark finally informed Arial if the movie was causing her to be uncomfortable they would leave, Arial agreed that she was uncomfortable and would like to leave. Clark was trying to be a perfect gentleman, they proceeded to leave immediately. Arial apologized, she explained she had no interest in that type of movie. Clark appeared to be content with Arial's decision, but actually he was not; he had other plans for that evening, now they were ruined.

Arial and Clark dated for approximately a year, then he asked her to marry him, and of course she replied with a yes. During this year they dated Arial saw all the signs of a mental and emotional relationship. Someone was finally giving her attention, she craved for attention, whether it was good or bad; someone was interested in her.

There were numerous signs of abuse, extreme jealousy, he demanded that he should be her only interest. Clark demanded her to appear perfect, but that curly hair, well, curly hair does what it wants to do. He would voice his opinion concerning the way she appeared. Usually, he was very demeaning, her hair was inappropriate, she was dressed in a way that was not becoming, there was always something wrong. She chose to ignore his sarcasm, she thought, there must be something he admires; he was still coming around. She had absolutely no idea what her life would consist of if she married this man.

The jealousy was probably the worst, if she looked in any direction; other than straight at him, she was eyeing another man. At the time Arial thought this was sweet. What she did not realize was how threatening this would become. Arial had lived her entire life remotely isolated. She basically had no friends, except for one. She had no experience with boys, she had only been on two dates before she met Clark. She was quite, no backbone whatsoever. The immediate attention she received from Clark swept her off her feet!

The relationship Clark and she had was basically how she grew up. This was all she knew, this was normal to her. Her dad had always treated her mother badly, and her mother allowed it. She honestly thought life was supposed to be that way.

Clark, finally after months of dating, squirmed his way into her panties. It was only a thirty second adventure, but Arial cried for hours. When Clark took her home that night, she was a mess. She knew she had to get past her parents, she had to clean up. She managed to hurry to the bathroom without their knowledge. She was safe this time, but she was frightened. Sex, she thought was overrated, it was not worth the time and effort it took her to clean up.

A couple of months passed, the sex continued, and Arial could have cared less about it. One night they were sitting in the car talking, and

Clark suggested they break-up, this was a shock to Arial, but not enough to cause tears. She sat quietly beside Clark and then she said, "that would probably be best, we will be miserable together if one does not have the desire to be together. It is because of the sex, isn't it? Clark replied, "partly." Arial opened the car door and proceeded to get out, Clark was not expecting this, he expected her to cry and beg. The reaction he received was not what he wanted. He was so sure of himself, but he was unpleasantly fooled. As Arial tried to exit the car Clark reached for her arm, this alarmed him to the point he changed his mind immediately. He said he wanted to try and resolve any issues they had. Stupidly, Arial agreed. Arial was so naive, if only she had continued with this attitude, her life and marriage would have been so much healthier.

On January, 3rd 1967 they married and life for Arial slowly spiraled downward. Arial was not allowed to leave the house without Clark's permission. She did try it at first, but she paid deeply emotionally. Clark would get mad and Arial would not have a clue as to why. She would beg him to explain to her what she had done, he never acknowledged her presence, he totally ignored her. This emotional abuse, Clark would deliberately prolong for a minimum of two weeks. He never spoke, touched, or acknowledged that she even existed. Arial's nerves were shattered, she was constantly afraid, she never knew what would set him off. She would beg daily, regardless of how desperate Arial appeared Clark seemed to be more determined not to break his silence. Arial continued to do everything for Clark, she carried his plate of food to him, she selected his clothes, started his bath, prepared his lunch for work; whatever she thought might help, she did it. Nothing produced a positive outcome.

Clark was determined to have full control over Arial, he was aware of her insecurities, and that she was very submissive. He used this knowledge to the maximum. Arial was treated as if she was dirt under his feet. Clark made Arial feel worthless, she felt like dirt beneath his feet. The mental abuse he dished out on her not only made her feel like dirt, but that he was purposely trying to grind her into the earth.

Arial was always alone, Clark had many sports he enjoyed participating in, none of which included Arial. She was not allowed to leave the house when he was out frolicking with his friends. He would allow her to see his mother and dad, they only lived two houses away. She definitely was not allowed to visit her parents, this was not a real issue with Arial, she did not care to be around her dad, it was just the principal of it. Clark had instilled an overwhelming fear within Arial, so she complied with his demands. She put forth every effort to do as he demanded; it really did not matter how perfect Arial was, Clark's attitude never wavered. He honestly did not care how depressed Arial became, or how much she cried or begged, he would not give an inch.

After a year of belittling, Arial was pregnant, she was deliriously happy, Clark, well he was not as thrilled. One day Clark wanted to visit a friend, Arial was allowed to join him, but only because the man was married. Arial was elated, she wanted to share her news concerning her pregnancy with her remote friend. Clark was furious, he instructed Arial not to mention the baby, he was tired of hearing about it. This hurt Arial's feelings so bad, was he ashamed of her and the baby? She was only in her second month, but she knew not to mention it, she would pay dearly if she did. Arial did not mention one word, but the news of the pregnancy had spread through the grapevine. Her friend mentioned it first, but Arial only acknowledged that she was pregnant, that was it, not another word. Her friend could see the fear on Arial's face, so she dropped the subject.

Clark's mother was thrilled with the news; she purchased Arial two maternity outfits. Arial was delighted, but Clark had no desire to even view the outfits. Those nine months seemed to take two years, Arial wanted this baby so much, she really thought that once the baby was born Clark would change. Arial was in for a rude awakening.

This bundle of joy only added to Arial's workload. Arial loved caring for her first son, so much so, she spoiled him terribly. This was a mistake, but Arial did not care, this child was all she had, and she loved him so much. He was the joy of her life.

Six months later Arial became pregnant again, Clark had very little to say about it. She really did not care what his opinion was concerning the pregnancy, he had received the enjoyment, she had to carry the baby and give birth. Another boy, Arial desperately wanted a girl, but as soon as that beautiful little baby was placed in her arms, it did not matter. Two and one-half years later she was pregnant, another boy, she was still happy with that bundle of joy. When she announced she was pregnant with the third child, Clark wanted her to have an abortion, which she defiantly refused. This caused turmoil, he did not speak to her for two weeks, Arial did not care if he ever spoke to her again, she would not have an abortion. Arial's children were the only reason she remained married to Clark. The first two pregnancies were planned, the last two just happened. Then came the fourth pregnancy, Clark was furious, abortion, abortion, abortion!!! Once again Arial refused, that started a rampage; she just ignored him, she was well aware of the actions that were going to happen. Clark did it again, almost solitary confinement, no talking, just complete silence. Arial's children were the only people she had to talk to. They were such little people, with a very limited vocabulary, but they gave her so much happiness, she thought at the time they were all she needed. She was wrong. All adults need an outlet, some way to express themselves to someone who will comprehend what is being said. Clark had no desire to talk to Arial about any subject, if Arial tried to start a conversation, Clark's statement was that he did not want to talk, and he would leave the room or the house. There Arial was alone, with four children. She had so much resentment towards Clark, the love was gone, but she had four children she was determined to raise with their father. This meant she would have the full responsibility of raising their children. Clark was never home, he did work, that was the only positive thing she could ever say about him. When Clark was not working he was with his friends, enjoying life to the fullest. There was no allotted time in his schedule that included his family. Clark, to this day does not realize that his family would have provided so much more happiness and contentment than all of his friends combined. He lost the joy of watching his three boys play sports, and his daughters' dance recitals. The pride a parent feels as they watch their children grow and mature each year gives more satisfaction and pleasure than anyone can imagine.

# Chapter Eight

## Tara's Pregnancy

After Arial's second child was born, Eloise, Arial's mother called to ask her if she would take Tara to the doctor. Arial could hear the hesitation in her mother's voice, she knew something was wrong and she was correct. Tara was pregnant, and she was only fourteen years old. Tara's mother suggested an abortion, Tara adamantly said no.

Arial made the doctor's appointment with her own obstetrician. The appointment date arrived, Arial dreaded this; Tara was only fourteen years old, a child herself. Tara was mature for her age, she had lived a vivid fourteen years; always into something. Arial drove to Tara's house, out the door she came, smiling. Arial smiled back, this was a child coming towards her car. Her stomach was flat, Arial assumed that Tara was only a couple of months into her pregnancy; Arial was in for a shock! Tara had felt the baby moving, she had not informed anyone, this was her secret.

The nurse called Tara's name, she just got up and proceeded toward the nurse alone, as if she had done this many times before. There was no fear within Tara, she had a positive attitude about everything in life. Arial remained in the waiting room, she was concerned about her sister. Tara was too young to be pregnant, we knew who the father was, it was

Don. Tara had been seeing this man for at least two years, he was a man, he was five years older than Tara. At first sight Tara was head over heels in love with Don. Everyone made fun and laughed at Tara each time she said she would some day marry Don. Arial was almost certain that day had arrived.

A while passed as Arial sat trying to read a magazine, gazing toward the nurses desk, wondering how much longer it would be. Maybe Tara was not really pregnant, that would be a blessing. Tara's body had not fully developed to the point that it was mature enough to carry a baby. She would be high risk; Tara appeared to be happy, but she did not have any inclination as to what a child would do to her very young life.

Finally the nurse called for Arial to come to the doctor's office, oh dear Lord, Arial did not want to go, she forced herself. Tara was already seated, and then Arial sat down. Dr. Sanford knew Arial, he had just delivered Arial's second child several months before. Dr. Sanford sat quietly for a moment, and then came the ultimate surprise. Tara was in her sixth month, Arial was flabbergasted, and she made it known that she did not believe it. Tara was so small, no visible signs of a pregnancy, much less well into her sixth month. Dr. Sanford assured Arial and Tara that he was positive. Arial was dumb-founded, but Tara did not appear to be surprised. Arial asked Tara if the baby was moving? Of course Tara said yes. The doctor assured each of them that the pregnancy so far was fine.

Then came the issue of insurance, which Tara did not have. Dr. Sanford suggested the health department, Tara and Arial were totally against this suggestion. Dr. Sanford explained that Tara would receive the exact quality of care at the health department as she would in his office. He further explained that he was the health department's doctor. She would only see him, this eased Arial's apprehensions. Arial trusted Dr. Sanford completely.

Dr. Sanford made all the arrangements for Tara's first appointment at the health department. Arial went with Tara for her first appointment, now this was what they hated, going to the health department gave the appearance that the mother was a floozy, and Tara was not. It also meant she did not have the money to pay a doctor in a private practice. Most of the mothers were young and alone, and by being there conveyed the message that each of them were very poor. They were poor, both Tara and Arial, but, they did not want the world to know it. Arial's life was better than Tara's, at least Arial had insurance, she never had to go to the health department. Arial considered herself very lucky. She would have been embarrassed if she had not had insurance, she definitely did not want to go to the health department. Arial did have just a little too much pride, Tara did also, but she as always could handle it.

Tara began her prenatal vitamins; she was to return in one month. Tara's stomach went from flat to big almost overnight. She did return for the next monthly visit, all was well; but that would be her last visit.

During this six week time span, Tara and Don had to make a decision. Tara was only fourteen years old and Don was nineteen years old. Don's mother came to Eloise to talk to her about the possible marriage. She was not against Tara, but she needed to explain some things concerning Don. She tried to explain that Don was not totally mentally correct. She did not know exactly what was wrong with Don but she wanted Tara's mother to understand that something was not quite right concerning Don's mental status. Tara was furious; she thought that Don's mother did not want them to marry, but that was not the reason, she honestly was concerned about her son.

Don's mother's apprehensions were ignored. Don was old enough to marry without parental consent, but Tara needed her mother's consent. Eloise did not want to give her consent, but she felt that was the only choice she had. Eloise thoughts were, what will the neighbors say or think? Eloise had more pride than most mother's and wives could ever have. She wanted things to remain silent as always. She assumed that if Tara and Don married everything would be in a nice quite place. She did not stop and think that all the neighbors and family members could count. Tara was well into her sixth month, a person did not have to be a rocket scientist to count three months.

It was not a shot gun wedding; all parties agreed it would be best for the baby. The marriage was kept hush-hush, Tara's dad was not informed concerning anything. He was told after the fact, but even that bastard was not stupid, he knew instantly that something was amiss. He actually kept his mouth shut for once in his life. He was positive that Tara was pregnant, no one had to inform him; Tara's stomach blew up like a balloon almost overnight.

Tara was very naïve about this pregnancy; she like all women did not know what to expect, this was her first baby and she was still a child herself. Tara was about seven and one half months, life was good, Don and she were doing well with the marriage and she thought she had six more weeks to go, surprise! One day she was walking towards her mother-in-laws house, she felt water running down her legs. She thought that she was peeing in her pants, she tried to rush, but it seemed the faster she moved; the wetter she was. Tara had heard about the water breaking, but she did not consider this, she had six weeks before her due date. She arrived at her mother-in-laws house in a frenzy, racing for the bathroom, very embarrassed. The water did not stop, it continued to tinkle, everyone noticed her stomach was smaller. Tara's mother-in-law instantly knew that Tara's water had broken. This caused great concern, it was too early for the baby. Tara was rushed to the hospital, everyone hoping this could be stopped. That was not possible, that little baby was determined to enter the world, and she did at three pounds and six ounces. Yes, it was a girl, so tiny; she could be held in the palm of a hand.

# Chapter Nine

## Depression and Marriage

Tara and Don had two more children during their somewhat turbulent marriage. Tara was a wonderful mother, even at the age of fourteen, the natural nurturing instinct was abundant. A child raising a child, that was it; but Tara did well.

Don's mental condition was not very noticeable when he was young, but as each year passed, the depression became very noticeable, especially to Tara. Tara truly loved Don, but she was so high-strung. She felt sorry for Don, she understood that he was sick, but there were times when she would lose control, she would scream at Don, even hit him. Don loved Tara also; he was very dependent upon her. Tara was the only person Don could talk to about his feelings or thoughts. Their life continued, Tara basically raised the children, Don was there in body but his mind was always somewhere else. During their twenty-five year marriage Don was repeatedly admitted to different mental facilities. He was diagnosed with manic-depression or bi-polar disorder. The depression part of the disease was by far the more prevalent. He was all alone in his own little world, he did work, but that was only possible with therapy and medications. He could not function even somewhat normally without the medications. Don's depression was almost as if he had fallen as low as possible and there was no way out. The depression lasted far longer than the manic phase. The manic phase was a feel good high, he felt normal. Don would do yard work, he and Tara would go shopping; Tara loved life when Don was in a manic phase. Overtime the depression totally took over Don's mind.

The children were grown, only the youngest child remained at home. For Tara life with Don was barely tolerable. She had to work, but Don's depression had spiraled to the bottom. He was not able to work, each day his depression appeared to increase in intensity. Their children did not understand their dad's illness, they did not understand the depression, the sadness, no verbal communication with them, no social time, and he needed to be alone almost constantly. Tara would just say their dad was sick, and not be mean or hateful to him. As teenagers they tried, but occasionally they would lose control and say or do hateful things to him. Don never responded, Tara would have to take control of the situation, these three children did not question their mother.

Don's mental health was declining rapidly; Tara could see the decline daily. The depression seemed to amplify, but his actions were the opposite, he paced continuously, frantically, normally he would depart to the bedroom and lay across the bed. It was different this time, he was so anxious, she could see the aggravation he felt. Don could not understand why his mind was the way it was. Why him, he would not wish this on anyone, but why him? The medications were not controlling his symptoms, in fact he was to the point of suicide, he had planned to take his own life when his youngest son, Tony, went on his graduation trip. He did not want Tony to be home to witness his suicide. Tara was so concerned she placed all the guns in the safe, she was the only one that knew the combination.

Tara returned from work, Don was well past the stage of saneness, and he knew this. He went to Tara and explained to her if she could ever help him, do it now; take him to the state mental hospital. Tara was shocked, if Don asked her to take him to the state hospital, she knew his mental state was worse than it had ever been, and it had been bad; but never this torturous. She immediately assisted him to the car, it was dark and this was at least a fifty mile drive. The drive was hectic, Don was speaking so erratically, no form of any normal context, and Tara thought that Don had finally entered a place that he may never return from. She was frightened for him, she loved him, and she would do whatever she could to help him.

Don and Tara arrived at the hospital late, but there were doctors available 24/7. Don freely admitted himself, by law he was to remain for seventy-two hours, even if self-admitted. Don was admitted and Tara remained in the lobby as Don was being evaluated. Tara always said that crazy people were drawn to her, during her wait in the lobby, she was surrounded by numerous patients. They wanted to talk to her, nothing in particular, just talk. She sat patiently as each patient spoke, she tried to respond with the correct words, just a few words she hoped would make them feel better.

The doctor returned and shooed the patients away, he needed to speak with Tara. His first question was, how long had they been married? Tara's response was twenty-five years. The doctor was tremendously surprised! He explained to Tara that it was very unusual for this type of marriage to last twenty-five years. Don's condition was severe, and for the majority of marriages there was a divorce. The sane spouse simply could not endure the chronic highs and lows of this type of marriage. He applauded her strength, love and loyalty to Don. He went on to say that she was an exceptional woman.

Don was admitted and Tara returned home. It was late when she arrived home, so she went straight to bed without informing anyone about Don. The following morning Tara called Arial to fill her in on everything that had happened. Arial was not surprised, she knew that Don's condition had declined. She was surprised that Don asked to be admitted. Tara sounded relaxed, not stressed. She was worried about Don but she was happy that he was not at home. This would be the only time she had to really rest. She desperately needed the rest, between work and Don; she was exhausted. Don demanded so much of her time and energy. The majority of Tara's day was devoted to Don, listening to his constant chatter; Tara was the only person that Don could or would talk to. He would talk endlessly about why his brain functioned incorrectly. He frequently told Tara that it seemed as if a light bulb turned on within his brain, but he did not understand the light bulb, why a light bulb? The depression had deepened to the point that Don very seldom spoke, if someone other than Tara came into a room; Don would rise and return to the bedroom, he could be alone there; alone with the door closed, he was in a separate world, he would sleep or think about himself; or how he could make himself feel better. There was no way out of his world, and he did not understand this. He wallowed in self-pity with suicidal thoughts. He wanted to die, he knew this was his only way he would recover, but he wanted to go to heaven; he was sane enough to realize that suicide would send him straight to hell. Quite frequently Don was at rock bottom, these were the times when Don did not consider heaven or hell, he just wanted to die, but he never developed enough nerve to complete the act of suicide.

Tara's rest and relaxation would be short lived, Don had been calling from the hospital; one patient was constantly trying to get into Don's bed. Arial instructed him to report the incident and ask to be moved. Don did as Tara requested, but with no results. Tara had to return to work on Sunday and she felt more relaxed than she had in a long time.

Tara had to work a twelve hour shit, approximately half way through her shift she received a phone call. It was her mother-law, Don had called and he wanted to return home, the man was still trying to get into Don's bed. Don's mother would never had proceeded to retrieve Don without Tara's consent. Tara agreed, but she chose to remain at work; his mother and dad drove to the hospital to pick him up. When Don and his parents returned, Don remained at his parents' house until Tara arrived home. It would be hours before Tara returned home, and Don was desperate for her to return. His parents watched and worried as Don paced throughout the house. He spoke very few words, if his parents attempted to talk to him; usually they received no response. They also wanted Tara to make a hasty return; their knowledge of helping Don was very limited. Tara was the only person Don could relate to and this was so difficult for Tara. Don's parents thought that when Tara did arrive home, Don's condition would improve.

Finally, Tara was home, Don's parents were elated, and Don instantly rose from the chair and hurried across the yard. Tara was not as thrilled to be home as everyone else was; she knew what was ahead, the constant talking and she was so tired. She did not have the strength to endure even one more day of this, but this was her only choice.

Don followed her into the house and it began, she wanted to scream; but she refrained from going overboard. He told her in great detail about the man trying to get in bed with him. Tara fully understood his concerns and she explained this to him. Don continued to talk rampantly, he was going to drive Tara crazy! Tara was listening but she was also trying to tune him out, unfortunately that did not work. Tara was puttering around, trying to function without going mad. Then she heard Don speaking important things, like the doctors changed his medicine. Don was very fickle about his medications, he did not like change. He was frightened about any new side effects that could possibly occur. Tara immediately began to listen earnestly to every word, Don had not been swallowing the new medications. The nurse would exit the room and Don would spit them into the toilet. He had practiced well at learning how to trick the nurses. The nurses did not have a clue that he was spitting the pills out. So, for over two days Don had no medications in his body at all. Tara knew his demeanor was more desperate now than before he went to the hospital. This frightened Tara, Don had been without medication for over forty-eight hours, and she was well aware of his fragile condition. His actions, body language, and speech had accelerated to a stage that truly terrified Tara. She had never been frightened of Don, but things had changed.

Tara immediately gathered Don's regular medicines, he took them without hesitation. He totally trusted Tara, whatever she requested he did it quickly. These medicines would not help Don for at least a few days. Tara knew there was nothing more she could do, except listen. She was so tired, she had worked a twelve hour shift; and then to come home to Don, well she was beyond exhaustion. She also had to work the following morning, she explained this to Don, he was deeply disappointed that she had to go to bed and work the next morning. Tara felt sad, but she had to work, Don had not worked in quite a while. They were from paycheck to paycheck, their small amount of savings had been depleted. Every factor in their life had been loaded and placed on Tara's shoulders, the load was almost more than she could carry.

She had to rest, she asked Don not to wake her, and he did not, he let her sleep through the night. Don did not sleep, his mind was in turmoil, so much confusion, he paced and lay on the sofa for short periods of time, up and down, constantly through the night. He heard the clock's alarm, it was time for Tara to get up. He did not want her to leave, but he was still sane enough to realize she must work. Don loved Tara so much, the need for her was probably greater than the love he felt for her.

Tara had to speed things up this morning, she did not have time to listen to Don, and she made this clear to him. Finally she left for work, Don was alone, and he also was frightened within his self. Don's youngest son was asleep; Tony was not an early riser. If Tony had been up, he would not have listened to his dad's constant rambling. Don's children had never been as close to their dad as they were to their mother.

# Chapter Ten

## Don's Return Home

This day would be the longest day Don had experienced in his life, and the events that would occur would destroy so many lives. Don wandered around throughout the day, he walked from his parents' house back to his house continuously. He spoke very little, but his parents were frightened, they had never viewed Don in this manner. Don was always depressed, except for the occasional manic high. This was different from the usual Don. He was so filled with anxiety, panic, and he wanted Tara home. He would not eat, the anxiety and pacing prevented him from eating. His parents could see the aggravation and anxiety on his face. They knew this was not normal, normally, all his life, sadness was the only expression they observed from his facial appearance. They had no inclination of how severe Don's mental condition had spiraled. They were frightened, but they had no idea the events this day would bring.

The day progressed so slowly for Don, even for his parents; they wanted and needed Tara at home, finally, about seven-forty five that evening Tara arrived home from work. Once again she was so tired, and she dreaded coming home. This day, she had decided; she was going to bed early, regardless of Don's condition. She actually needed two nights of sleep straight, instead of one. She did not know how much more she could endure, if this continued, Tara would be as crazy as Don. Tara remembered what the doctor had said at the hospital, most marriages like theirs did not last, now she understood why, Don had never been to this place with his mental illness, and she did not understand how to go forward from here.

Don was anxiously waiting; he needed to talk to her so desperately, Tara was nervous, as she drove into the driveway, her fingers were tapping the steering wheel briskly. There he was; as soon as Don came into view, Tara knew that his condition had declined so much more than it was the night before. God, she thought; what am I going to do? Don's pacing back and forth had increased to an extremely rapid speed, he was talking constantly, harsher, more defiant than yesterday. Tara was more than a little concerned, she was scared. She had never felt these emotions concerning Don's illness, she had always had the upper hand, but tonight was so different. Tara normally ate something when she returned from work, not tonight, she was nauseated. It was not from a sickness, but from escalating anxiety and fear. She sat and watched and listened to each word Don spoke. The words he spoke were slightly incoherent and had very little reasoning to them.

Their youngest son was at home, but of course he was nineteen years old, and he wanted to go out for the evening. Tony did not understand the severity of his dad's condition, he knew he was sick, but his need for a pleasurable evening outweighed the need his mother had for him to remain at home. Tara asked Tony not to leave, to please stay at home with her. His dad had never hurt his mother, and he was certain she would be alright that night. So, Tony left, leaving his mother very vulnerable.

Tara's brother, Kendall called Tara about 10:30 P.M. to assure himself that she was alright. Tara informed Kendall about Don's condition, he could sense the anxiety in Tara's voice, she was very uneasy. Kendall was more than a little concerned, he asked if she needed him to come to her house, but of course; Tara said, no, she would be alright. To this day sixteen years later, Kendall regrets not going to Tara's house, but he like everyone else never expected Don to ever hurt Tara.

Tara's conversation ended with Kendall, she continued to observe Don closely, his behavior was never bizarre, in their entire marriage; Tara had not seen this type of behavior from Don. Normally Don was in a deep depression, quite, withdrawn, and in a place that was only his. He never let anyone into his world except Tara, Tara loved Don, but she did not enjoy his world, but she was married to this man; and that meant assisting him with all of his needs.

Tony, their son had left for the evening and Kendall had called and Tara was ready to retire for the day. She was so sleepy; she could hardly keep her eyes open. She would drift a sleep sitting straight up. Don's state of mind did not care, he needed to talk. Although Tara was frightened because of Don's extremely erratic behavior, she was determined to go to bed. She gave Don explicit instructions, she needed to sleep and he was not to wake her. She explained to Don they would talk the next day, Don agreed, but he honestly did not know if he could wait until the next day. His anxiety level was through the roof, but he assured Tara that he would not wake her, he would let her sleep.

Tara was asleep almost immediately, she was so tired, and her brain went to a deep sleep quickly. Don was alone with his mixed up thoughts, he remembered what Tara had said, and he did the best he could to comply with her wishes. He paced the house, moving quickly from one sitting position, in one chair to another. He could not sit still, his thoughts were changing constantly from one thought to maybe a hundred in just seconds. Don could not contain himself any longer, no one knows exactly what time Don reached his limit, or what time he decided to wake Tara.

# Chapter Eleven

## The Day of a Nightmare

Arial, Tara's older sister had jury duty the following day. She was sleeping in as long as possible. Clark, Arial's husband was up, getting ready for work. It was early, but the sun was already shining, the light peeping through the blinds began to awaken Arial. She did not want to go for jury duty; she trusted that she would be excused. It was about 6:30 a.m. The phone rang, Arial was a little startled, she did not like for the phone to ring at night or early morning, it usually meant something critical had occurred. She continued to lay quietly, Clark had answered the phone. She wondered who would be calling this early in the morning, curiosity finally got the best of her, she slowly sat up, she felt dread, but she proceeded toward the hall.

There was not one sound to be heard, it was unnatural, the silence in the house. Arial walked cautiously toward the living room, there was Clark standing at the phone crying! He did not speak until Arial spoke, Arial asked, "Who called?" Clark responded by saying, "It was Kendall". Arial could feel the anxiety building, she grasped the fact that something was terribly wrong. Arial asked, "What did he want?" Clark continued to cry, and suddenly Clark said, "Tara is gone". Arial could feel her stomach began to quiver, Arial asked, "Where did she go"? Arial's body began to tremor, Clark had not answered her yet, quietly he said something, Arial screamed and ran to the kitchen corner and collapsed to the floor. She was uncontrollable, Clark could not calm her, he tried but she pushed him away. The words that Clark spoke were more than Arial's mind could accept. At that moment and until this day, Arial brain blocked those three words to protect her, she still does not remember what Clark said. Later Clark explained it to her, he said, "Tara is dead"!

Arial's next thought was her mother; she had to call to reassure herself that her mother was alright. Eloise, her mother was very distraught, Arial assured her mother that she would be there quickly.

Arial had to dress, she did so quickly, she half dressed, later she was not sure if she had brushed her teeth, but she really did not care. Clark and she drove across town, it seemed to take an eternity; but they finally arrived. It was a warm day, the family was sitting outside on the porch, some were crying, Arial was amazed at the calmness of her mother. She appeared to be so sad, she had been crying, but now she sat calmly in a chair. Everyone remained silent when Arial arrived; she stood staring at each of them, then she screamed, "What happened?" They did not have an answer, Arial slammed her fist against the post, to no avail, she only hurt her fist, the post remained solid.

Suddenly Arial remembered she had jury duty, she screamed at Clark that he needed to go to the courthouse and inform someone that she would not be present! She had no intention of appearing, and Clark would have to do something. Clark left immediately, when he returned, he explained that he had to speak to three different people, to get Arial excused. Of course, Arial's jury duty was rescheduled. She did not care, she just knew that she was not going!

Arial stood quietly and stared at her family, they were sitting there, of course they were upset, but they seemed to be lost, they were observing

Arial; not sure of what her next reaction would ensue. Arial and Tara had been so close, more so than most sisters. There closeness was unique, they worked together, and they went to the doctor together, they went shopping on a weekly basis, talked on the phone for hours, well, they did everything together. The entire family knew that Tara's death might destroy Arial.

Arial had stood quietly as long as she could; she thought the family had totally lost their minds. She announced to each of them that she was going to Tara's house, well, this caused a disruption. They explained to Arial there was nothing she could do, this set Arial off, she explained that they could sit there on their asses if that was what they chose to do, but she was going! Arial turned to Clark, with such anger, either he would drive her, or she would drive herself! She used some very unique words, these words enticed Clark to move his lazy butt extremely fast. There was no way Clark would allow Arial to drive the car alone in her present state of mind which consisted of anxiety and rage. Clark and Arial drove up the street, Clark knew they needed gas, but he dreaded telling Arial. He knew this was going to piss her off, but he had to tell her. When he did he received the response he expected, a rampant rage. Arial commented this was his fault, he constantly waited until the tank was on E before he refilled. Arial knew stopping for gas would only prolong her arrival. She was having irrational thoughts, this might not be real, maybe there had been a mistake with the communication; if she could get there maybe she could prevent whatever was occurring. Arial, at this point simply could not accept the fact that Tara was dead, she refused to believe it,

They approached the road that Tara lived on, they made the turn; the first thing they saw were police cars with their lights flashing. The closer they got they saw that Tara's yard was taped off with yellow paper. There were policemen walking quickly over the yard. The rescue squad was there with their lights flashing continuously.

Clark and Arial quickly exited the car and hurried into the house. They were at Tara's in-laws house. They entered the house and there was complete silence, once again, no one knew what to expect from Arial. Arial went to her sister's children, the three of them were sitting in a room that had a window facing their mother's house. Lela, Tara's daughter, was crying uncontrollably, nausea so intense she was vomiting. Tara's two sons were to the point they appeared to be numb. Their eyes were red and swollen from crying. Arial asked what had happened, but no one seemed to have any knowledge, except that Tara was dead!

Arial and Tara's children had a clear view from the window. Arial observed the scurrying of the law enforcement officials, they had evidence tags all over the yard, God only knew how many were inside the house. Arial wanted and needed to see her sister, but she knew that would be impossible. Quietly they continued to watch every movement, then suddenly there was a stretcher, being carried out the door. They stopped for a moment. The stretcher carried what appeared to be a black vinyl bag that was zipped to the top. Arial's stomach began to quiver, nausea was beginning; she knew that Tara's small frail body was enveloped within that black bag. Arial was so concerned, it was dark inside that bag; and she knew Tara was frightened. Arial's brain was having such bizarre thoughts, she knew that Tara did not comprehend what was occurring. She did not know why she was zipped up in a black bag and it was dark; Arial knew that Tara was very frightened, and she wanted desperately to go to her and comfort her, but Arial was sane enough to realize this would not be allowed. She felt so lost, what could she do to undo this tragedy? Arial's mental status was beginning to decline, the thoughts that were roaming inside her brain were disturbing, but to Arial they were normal. A few moments later, the paramedics began to secure the stretcher, and then they began to push the stretcher toward the rescue vehicle; they were going to take her away! Where were they taking her? Arial was so disturbed, what were they going to do to her? They continued to escort the stretcher to the vehicle, then they raised the legs, lifted and positioned the stretcher inside. A few anxious minutes passed and they drove away. Arial and Lela, Tara's daughter were inconsolable.

A short time passed before the police arrived to inform the family that the crime scene investigation was complete. The police informed them that they could re-enter the house. That was it, no other information was given. At that time the police packed up their evidence and left. Arial was dumb-founded, not any information was revealed.

Arial did not have any desire to enter the house, she explained to Tara's children that she was leaving, they understood, they did not want to enter their mother's house, but they knew they had to.

Don, Tara's husband had killed Tara, his family remained in another room, and they had loved Tara as if she was their daughter. They were just as distraught as Arial's family was, but they remained silent; they did not want to cause an up roar because of something they might say that would be taken the wrong way. Arial suggested to Clark that they should leave, but the last words Arial spoke as she exited the house were, "someone needs to see about Don". Arial knew that Don was very sick mentally, and at this moment she was giving him the benefit of the doubt.

Clark and Arial returned to her mother's house, there they were, the entire family sitting on the porch, it appeared as if no one had moved. Everyone faces seemed to portray a look of being lost. No one was talking; their faces were tear-stained, solemn and so sad. Tara had been the ultimate sunshine of the family, she would go out of her way to help anyone, she induced laughter in anyone she spoke to. Tara also had a very poignant attitude, if you asked her a question, then you should expect to receive her opinion; so if you did not want the truth, do not ask. She did have a tendency to piss people off, but her personality was so delightful and inspiring, by the next day these same people were speaking to her once again. No one remained upset with Tara for more than one day. Most people, after some soul-searching, realized she was right. Tara was one of a kind, the good Lord above made only one Tara, then he discarded the mold. That was probably a good idea, she is irreplaceable.

Slowly Arial's family began to ask questions, and she had no answers. She only knew that Tara was dead and Don had killed her, other than that, the outcome was the same, and their knowledge of what had occurred was nil.

Arial's mother's health was declining; she was not physically able to assist with any preparations for the wake, everyone agreed that family and friends would meet at Eloise's house; with this decision in place, Eloise would not have to journey all over Kingston. This would allow her one night at home, everyone would come to her. Tara's children were fine with this arrangement.

Arial and Clark decide to return home, Arial was a total basket case, everyone could see this; her anxiety level was through the roof. Her aunt, was very concerned about Arial's condition, she had some anti-anxiety medicine; she offered Arial a few, but she only gave Arial one, the remaining ones she gave to Clark. Everyone was aware of the special closeness Tara and Arial had, and quite frankly they were concerned that Arial might swallow all the pills. No one knew how accurate their thoughts were.

They returned home, and then Arial realized that her four children had not been notified, frantically she began calling each of them, of course none of her children answered their phones. She called her nephews and begged them to go to her children's house. Of course they did as she asked. It was not long; her children began arriving; demanding answers. Arial did not have the answers they were demanding. The news concerning the death of their aunt was devastating to each of them. Tara had baby-sit for Arial on numerous occasions, her children loved their aunt Tara, Tara was full of crap with her own kids as well as Arial's. They loved her for her humor, her love of life, and the discipline they received from their aunt, which Arial approved of wholly. The love they felt for her was genuine and sincere. She was their favorite aunt.

Later that evening, Lela, Tara's daughter called Arial; to ask if she would like to assist them as they chose a plot and a casket. Of course Arial was honored to be asked, she immediately replied yes. Lela said they would meet the following morning at the cemetery, about ten o'clock.

Arial needed to call her mother, Eloise was hiding most of her emotions from the family, but Arial was concerned about any small amount of time she was left alone, which was infrequently. There was someone there almost constantly, even if it was only a neighbor. Eloise had tried to make it perfectly clear that she did not want or need anyone to stay with her at night, but that was only wishful thinking, she would not be left alone. Eloise had basically raised two of her grandsons; to them she was a mother. The youngest of the two was so devoted to his grandmother, he quickly and firmly informed her that he would sleep there for a few nights. Jock was his name and he politely informed her that she did not have a choice.

Arial needed rest, she was so agitated, words would spill from her mouth that made absolutely no sense. Her husband Clark and her children were at a loss as how to comfort her. She was constantly crying, jerking, she truly wanted everyone to go away, leave her alone, they almost refused to talk to her, each of them were frightened they would say inappropriate words. This seemed to set Arial into an uncontrollable rage, which included profuse language that was very inappropriate for Arial, and to make matters worse; Arial did not have any regards for anyone around her, or what their thoughts were concerning her language.

It was time for bed, Arial dreaded lying down, trying to sleep; Clark gave her one anti-anxiety pill hoping it would relax her just enough for her to sleep. Arial's brain and body were in a battle against each other.

Physically she was exhausted, but her brain was in turmoil. She lay in the bed thinking only about Tara, the inside of her body felt as if it was running at a terribly fast speed, and she apparently had no control. A few moments later, she heard Clark snoring, how could he sleep so easily? This irritated Arial, but there were a lot of things that irritated Arial where Clark was concerned. She really did not like him, much less love him.

She needed to sleep, there was such a large agenda the following day. She wanted to be a part of it, but there was dread associated with it. Clark slept sound throughout the night, but Arial's sleep was limited, she would drift off, wake up and wonder what the coroner was doing to Tara's tiny body. There had to be an autopsy, so her body was sent to Crowleigh, the state medical's office. Arial was frightened for Tara, this was her little sister, and God only knew what they were doing to her tiny body. Arial knew that Tara was dead, but she felt like Tara was scared. Arial received very little sleep, she woke frequently during the night, with the same thoughts roaming around inside her head.

Morning arrived too soon; the sun was barely peeking through the blinds, and Arial felt as if a truck had ran over her. She felt like a zombie, she sat on the side of the bed trying to open her eyes, her thoughts were all bungled together; she knew she had to move quicker. She needed to be at the cemetery by ten o'clock, Clark was up and dressed, but he had slept soundly through the night. He insisted on driving her to the cemetery, this aggravated Arial; she was not allowed to leave the house without Clark. She felt that she did not need his constant supervision, but it was out of the question, he was determined to escort her everywhere she went.

Arial finally dressed but she was dragging, she wanted to be a part of this, and she was so glad Tara's kids had included her, but the desire to move was gone, but she managed to gradually to get dressed. Clark was hurrying her, so she did speed up, she did not want to even hear him speak.

Clark and Arial were the last ones to arrive at the cemetery, but she was there, and that was all that mattered. Tony wanted a plot near the road, plus a tree near the plot. They discovered the perfect plot. Arial was there for support, not for her opinion, but she totally agreed with their decision. Arial thought the tree was great, Tara would have shade, this would help her remain cool. Tara loved warm weather, but sometimes she would get ticked off if it was a scorcher day. The plot Tara's children selected was exactly on the side of the road, and Arial knew that she would enjoy this. She would be able to see everyone that came by. Tara would love this; she had always wanted to know what was happening around her.

Then, someone mentioned purchasing a plot for Don, Arial was shocked. Don had killed their mother and they wanted to bury him beside her for all eternity! They looked at Arial, maybe for some sign of approval, but Arial just turned her head with no response. She knew this was not her decision, it was theirs, and theirs alone. Lela, Tara's daughter, knew without asking what Arial's opinion was, but these were their parents and at the time they like everyone else, they knew that something had went terribly wrong that night. Don loved Tara, and something mentally snapped within Don. They could not separate the two of them; it had always been mother and dad. It would be cheaper to purchase it now than later. Their emotions captured them, this was such a terrible time for them, and they let their emotions take over. Arial tried to achieve an appearance that revealed that it was okay, but Lela knew and she understood.

The next thing on the agenda was the florist; Lela asked Arial if she would go with her, of course Arial agreed. Arial wanted to order a flower, but Lela was deciding on the spray for the casket. Tara had always said that when she died she wanted yellow rose buds for her spray. It can be and was difficult to obtain enough yellow rose buds for a casket spray. Lela did prevail; the florist had to call several florists to obtain that large of an order. Arial ordered a white cross with a Bible. It required a huge amount of strength and courage to get these works of love accomplished. It seemed to weaken each of them, but that weakness may have been caused from not eating for two days.

A daughter lost her mother, the one person in her life that she loved and admired the most. A mother that was always there when needed, one that could listen without preaching, and a mother with an everlasting love that had never flickered.

A sister lost the only sister she had, the one person that she loved unconditionally, her only confidant, and her only true friend. A sister that if asked for an opinion, well, her honest opinion was given, good or bad.

Mother's and sisters are family members that can never be replaced, always cherish the time and the quality of that time. Everyone will die sooner or later, but that time is not known to anyone. Life is short, sometimes shorter than it should be, this is the unexpected ones, the ugly surprises in life that may cause a tremendous amount of grief and guilt left over from spits and spats. These spits and spats may seem important at the time, but afterwards they are so frivolous. A person cannot go back when all is over, it is simply too late!

# Chapter Twelve

## Tara's Wake

Arial and Lela went their separate ways, both were sick, nauseated and were in desperate need of rest and sleep. Neither had eaten since Tara died, they had so much guilt, their minds were just a little warped. They felt guilty if they even thought of eating, Tara could not eat, so how could they eat? The very thought of food caused both to become more stressed than they were. The guilt out-weighed their need for food, waves of anxiety increased as family members tried to put food in their mouth.

The day was ending, the next day was the wake, but before the wake; the family had to be at the funeral home at 2:00 P.M. to view the body. This was to make sure the family was satisfied with the appearance of Tara.

Arial was not prepared for any of those requirements, she had not fully accepted the fact that Tara was dead. Arial felt as if she had not spoken to Tara in a couple of days, sometimes she would sit and stare at the phone, hoping it would ring. Then she could answer the phone and she would hear Tara speak; then she would realize that she had the most horrible nightmare of her life! This never happened, Arial squandered that day sitting in the floor crying, her head was pounding, her heart was racing, and her body felt like a train soaring without brakes; no way to slow down.

It was time for bed, Clark was ready for bed; and of course he expected her to go also. Arial was not in the mood for an argument, so they retired for the night. Once again, Clark slept soundly, Arial slept in short intervals; never a deep sleep, the depth of sleep she needed for her body to begin recovering. Arial's body never completely recovered, especially mentally.

Oh God, there was sunshine, this meant Arial had to rise. What she really wanted was to sink into the mattress as far as it would take her, cover herself and never see the light of day ever again. There was a nudge, it was Clark; she had to get up soon, Arial also wished he would disappear from her sight, but God forbid; that would never happen! She finally gave up, and went to the kitchen, she needed coffee and about two packs of cigarettes, that might get her started. There he was, Clark waiting in the kitchen, he was constantly in view, if Arial needed to talk, well, he would disappear; he was not discussing Tara. Why, Arial did not know, he refused, he would walk away, he said he did not care to discuss it, but Arial actually needed someone to talk to, but Clark made it crystal clear that person would not be him.

The morning was almost over, Arial had to dress, she did not want to go to the funeral home, in her terribly mixed up brain, she thought if she did not go, all that had occurred would not be real. Clark was ready to go somewhere, so something had happened, it must be real. Reluctantly, Arial got dressed rather quickly, she looked a mess, but she was clean, that was good enough.

Clark and Arial were the last of the family to arrive, no one had entered, maybe they were waiting for her. Clark sat there watching Arial, she remained in her seat, she was not sure she could do this. Her sister was inside; this would be the first time Arial had seen her since she had died. Clark opened his door and proceeded to get out of the car. Arial was sitting still, quietly staring at the people waiting, the tears began to stream from her eyes, this was just the family, what would it be like tonight at the wake? She finally opened the car door, and forced herself to get out. She had to enter the funeral home, she was still hoping Tara was not in there, but she also knew that was wishful thinking. Slowly she walked toward the steps, she was beginning to hyperventilate, the closer she moved toward the door, she knew that she might pass out, this she did not want to do, Clark was trying to assist her, but Arial could not retrieve enough air, everyone was trying to help Arial, it took a few moments but Arial recovered enough to enter the funeral home. Clark remained with Arial; they could see the casket from outside the room. Arial stopped to steady herself, she had to step inside, and there were so many flowers, huge beautiful flowers surrounded the casket. Clark held her arm as they walked closer; then Arial saw the pink suit Tara was wearing, more tears that were uncontrollable began again, her body was jerking, but she continued. She saw that curly hair, but the closer she got she knew something was not right. The person laying in the casket did not have any resemblance to Tara. Arial knew it was Tara, but it was so upsetting to view this body. Tara's dentures were too large for her small mouth, but her children insisted that she have her dentures in. Arial's thoughts were roaming again, she bent down to kiss her and she whispered, "Tara, you do not look good". If Tara could have responded, she would have said, fix it! Tara had never worn make-up of any kind, so Lela decided that she would not want it now, that was a mistake. Her complexion appeared shallow, she had very dark circles under and around her eyes. Just a small amount of make-up would have worked wonders.

Tony, Tara's youngest son arrived, as he approached the casket, he lost all control. He was screaming, "This is not my mother, someone has made a mistake!" Tony was crying so intensely, it was difficult to understand the words he was speaking, except that he was adamant that this was not his mother! Everyone was trying to console Tony, but he was so mad, Arial tried to explain that it was the dentures.

The funeral director asked Arial to step aside with him; he asked if there was anything that he could do to improve Tara's appearance? Arial quietly explained that Tara's children did not want any make-up, and that was their decision; so everything was to remain the same. Tony was finally convinced that was his mother.

Arial was not satisfied with Tara's appearance at all, but it was not her decision, so she remained silent. The time had come for everyone to leave, they had to return at 6:00 P.M. for the wake, and that was not very long.

Clark and Arial left, they barely had enough time to return home and dress for the wake. Arial called her mother and asked if she wanted to ride with Clark and her to the wake. She had decided to ride in the family car, and that was fine with Arial. Arial's nerves were shot, she was not sure if she could acquire enough strength to relate to the many visitors she was sure would be present. Arial understood that her mother was trying to remain as calm as possible, but to hold this tremendous amount of grief within her was not beneficial for her mother's health. Eloise had a very bad heart, and the stress and anxiety could cause problems or damage. Arial certainly was not the best person to encourage her mother to relax and let the tears flow, because Arial was crying almost constantly. Arial felt as if the wake would allow her mother to let go, but she was not sure.

The wake began at 6:00 P.M., When Clark and Arial arrived at the funeral home, it had actually began. Family and friends arrived early; Clark and Arial were also early, a line of mourners had begun, and the line was exiting the door, so many people, wonderful people that had come to show their respect.

Clark and Arial entered and sat at their designated seats. Arial had to sit, she was so wobbly, she knew she could not stand. Lela, Tara's daughter was almost to the point of losing all control, she was crying, her hands were in a constant jerk. She spoke to very few people, she just nodded her head as an acknowledgement, mentally and physically, that was the only way she could respond.

Every visitor had a deep desire to touch Tara, but the funeral director had instructed Arial to please not rub her face or any skin showing, it required a lot of work to disguise the numerous wounds. Every one tried, but they could not resist the urge to touch or kiss Tara. Arial was probably the worst; she had to kiss Tara repeatedly and rub her hands. She would leave the casket and return immediately, she could not stay away from her sister. Arial's daughter-in-law, Renee, would constantly return to view Tara's body, she would say; just one more time over and over.

Arial was so tired, but people kept coming and coming, the line of visitors continued out the door, down the steps, and as far down the street as could be seen. The wake lasted longer than planned because of the increased amount of people that attended. It was far more than had been anticipated. When all the names were counted in the registrar, there were over one thousand names. The family was very appreciative for all the visitors, they were sure that Tara knew everyone in town. Flowers were sent from past employers, long forgotten friends, close friends, and of course a multitude from family members.

Finally, by ten o'clock, people were thinning out, the family was grateful, they were so tired. Arial was beyond exhausted, but she did not want to leave Tara alone, she knew Tara would be all alone in the dark, in Arial's mixed up thoughts Tara would be frightened! Arial was the last to leave, Clark was also tired, but Arial did not care; in the end it took every ounce of strength Arial could collect to walk out the door and leave Tara alone.

Clark and Arial arrived home late, but for Arial, sleep was difficult. Her body could not wind down. She was so concerned about Tara being alone in that dark room, Arial was convinced that Tara did not understand what had occurred or why she was lying in a casket. Arial was a mess mentally and physically, her thoughts were completely irrational; but Arial did not see them as being irrational; she assumed everyone felt the same way.

# Chapter Thirteen

## Tara's Funeral

Arial woke earlier than usual; it was still dark, this was the day of Tara's funeral. Tara wanted to be alone for a while, and she meant alone; she did not want to awaken Clark. If Clark was up she would still be alone, but she did not have any desire to see his face that morning. Arial quietly slipped from the bed, and tip-toed toward the kitchen, she started the coffee, sat at the table in the dark. She began to think of all the wonderful times Tara and she had experienced throughout their adult life. Their children were the most important possessions in their life. Their children were the most important accomplishments they had. They had disciplined not only their own children, but each other's.

Arial remembered when Tara and she actually were lost in a mall parking lot. It was hilarious at the time, as it was now, but it also brought tears, tears that were streaming down her cheeks, she could taste the salt as it reached her lips. Arial had drank at least three cups of coffee and smoked a half a pack of cigarettes, she knew those darn things were going to kill her sooner or later, but she kept on smoking.

The kitchen was getting lighter, she glanced toward the window, and the sun was rising; she knew she had plenty of time, so she poured one more cup of coffee and lit one more cigarette. She dreaded this day; it would be the last day she would ever see her sister. The day would be a very long day; one filled with tears, and wrecked nerves. Arial's anxiety level had never declined; she could only imagine what her character would be like later in the day.

She knew she had to wake Clark; she did not want to, she would rather attend her sister's funeral without him, but once again she knew this was wishful thinking. Clark was asleep and Arial's clothes were in the bedroom, she had no choice but to wake him. Reluctantly she made herself enter the bedroom, he was awake, and he was lying in bed quietly, she was sure he did not want to deal with her or this day any more than she did. Clark got up instantly, as he passed her he touched her shoulder, maybe that was a sign of affection, but Arial could have cared less. She wanted to be left alone.

Tara's funeral was at 2:00 P.M. but they had to be at Arial's mother's at 12:00, the final viewing was at 1:00 and Arial was dragging, as usual. Finally after half the morning had passed, Clark and Arial were dressed, but Arial's comprehension was screwed up. She simply could not wrap her brain around the fact that her only sister was dead, and today, she would be buried.

Clark and Arial finally on their way, Arial's mind and body had been in a battle all morning, both shattered and worn out, they seemed just to go along for the ride. Clark and Arial slowly drove through town, Arial was just watching the world go by. She watched as men and women walked the streets going to work, to lunch, or wherever they were going. The cars stopped at red lights, impatiently waiting for it to turn green. She only spoke to Clark one time, as she began to cry, she told him that the whole world was going about their daily routines, her sister was dead and no one cared. Arial wanted the world to stop, remember her sister, acknowledge her life and death, but she also knew that this would not occur. The world did not realize how much Tara would be missed, how much joy would be reduced every day without her dazzling personality. This made Arial so sad, almost mad, and to make matters worse, she received absolutely no response from Clark. He was driving the car that was it, his opinion did not have any substance at all. He had become a chauffeur, no chit chat; just a driver. Arial looked at Clark, he never moved his head, almost as if she was not even in the car. He had no familiarity dealing with a crazy woman, and that is what he thought Arial was; crazy.

They finally arrived at Arial's mother's house, everyone was to meet there and go to the funeral home together. Of course Clark and Arial were the last ones to arrive, they understood; they were aware that Arial was not altogether. Upon arrival, they had to leave immediately, time was running out, they needed to speed things up. They were on their way, Arial lost all control she had been trying to hold on to all morning, Clark immediately reached into his pocket to retrieve the anti-anxiety pills, Arial refused the pill, she knew this would be the last time she would see her sister on this earth, she wanted to be alert, not spaced out. She wanted to be fully aware of any minute thing that might need her attention. So deep in Arial's inner being, she was still praying that a mistake had been made, she desired this so, but she did not speak of it, the family thought she had already lost her mind. She knew that some of her mental thoughts could never be spoken verbally, these thoughts had to be a secret.

The funeral home was prepared for the final viewing; this would only last about thirty minutes. People rushed in to say a final farewell to Tara, all exited crying. The casket lid was lowered and fastened and the pall bearers, three of which were Arial's son's proceeded to lift and escort her body to the chapel. The family was seated, and the chapel was standing room only. The chapel was so full it could not allow anyone else inside, a large number of mourners remained outside in the scorching heat, no one left until the service was complete.

The casket stood in front of the pulpit, yellow rose buds cascaded from the top to the sides. Tara made it clear that her uncle Vance would perform the service, and of course mother's minister would assist. Arial's uncle Vance was to begin the service, and everyone knew that this would be the most difficult service he would ever perform. Tara was one of the most precious things on this earth to him. He rose from his chair and so humbly walked to the pulpit, tears were streaming down his cheeks; he was trying so hard, his voice was crumbling with each word he spoke. He only spoke a few sentences and he broke down, he had to discontinue for the moment. Their uncle Vance had been their favorite uncle forever. Tara had always instructed Arial that she did not want a long drawn out funeral, she said that people get tired and bored. She also did not want a pack of lies told to give her a better image, she wanted the truth told, just say she was a good old girl, just a few truths, but absolutely no lies. Maybe one or two songs, she loved, HOW GREAT THOU ART, she wanted that song sung by a dear friend of her mother's. Arial spoke to her uncle Vance before the service and he agreed, or at least he would try.

Their mother's minister rose to say a few words, and to give their uncle Vance time to recover. His, what was supposed to be a few words, was much longer. It was almost a preaching service, Arial knew that Tara was not pleased. Their uncle Vance had regained his composure, and everyone was thankful. He returned to the pulpit with fewer tears, but he did as Arial asked, it was honest and to the point, he highlighted Tara's many talents, her priorities in life, one was to do for others, love and cherish her children and to live a life that was strong, giving and caring.

Arial was listening carefully to each word her uncle had spoken, as she listened, she was also talking to Tara, Arial explained to Tara that the service may not have been the good old girl service, but it was pretty close, Arial felt as if Tara was happy with the service. There was one more function to be performed to complete the service, the graveside service, the one Arial dreaded the most. Everyone left the chapel, it was a terribly hot and humid day, but all of Tara's friends that could not get inside were still standing in the parking lot, tears and perspiration mixed together was not good. These people loved Tara so much, she had touched so many peoples lives' they considered it an honor just to have known her. Her life was shortened abruptly, no one knew why; there was sorrow, confusion, and the grief would be long lived.

Famous people pass and the other famous attend their funeral just because they were famous, some really care, but most do not, they are there sometimes to be seen. Tara's life and death was an exceptional one. She was treasured by so many people, her presence on this earth left an ever-lasting impression with so many. She will never be forgotten, her memory will live on in the minds of each person she touched.

Shortly after the chapel was empty, Tara's casket was rolled out to the funeral home car, carefully they lifted and placed the casket inside the back. Arial's brain was working overtime, she was positive that Tara could feel every movement, she could hear every sound and word that was being spoken.

Everyone entered their cars and waited for the procession to begin, it was not far to the cemetery, maybe a couple of miles, but it was too fast for Arial, she was not ready for this final good-bye. This time Arial did not hesitate, she immediately exited the car and walked to the gravesite and took her seat. She sat there staring at the casket, the sunshine, the yellow rose buds, each item Tara had requested had been completed. Arial was speechless, she remained quiet and still, but she continued to stare straight ahead, she stared at that green carpet laying under Tara's casket, they could not fool Arial, she knew there was a six feet hole beneath that green carpet. She also was aware that after the service that Tara's body would be lowered into that hole. Somewhere in Arial's mixed up mind she assumed that she was the only person there that was aware of the next step, and the next step. She carefully inspected the faces of the people sitting around, they all wanted to be there, but they were lost, at that moment Arial's reasoning was that all these people had no idea of what was next. She had an immense desire to scream to each person that Tara knew what was happening to her, that she was scared. Arial was concerned for Tara only, the fear she must be feeling. Most of these people only had thoughts about their loss and how their life could possibly go on without her. Arial had these same thoughts, but her fear of the unknown seemed to overpower any rational thoughts. Arial was very sick, but she was not recognizing the symptoms.

The graveside service was very short, just a few words spoken by their uncle Vance, Then a very short prayer and it ended. Most stood up and slowly walked past Tara's casket, just to touch one last time. Arial remained seated, Clark also remained seated; he was anxious about leaving Arial even for a second. Some people began to leave, but Arial was not prepared to leave Tara yet. Clark just waited silently, trying to give Arial all the time she needed. Finally Arial realized that she had to leave. She knew they would not proceed until everyone had left the cemetery.

Arial knew what was next; they would remove the carpet they were using to disguise that hole, and slowly lower Tara into the ground. Arial was certain that Tara would feel every movement, every thud and swish of the casket. Arial was very unstable when she stood up, her head felt like it was swimming, the nausea in her stomach was almost overwhelming. She felt as if she might pass out, Clark had her arm; he was actually gentle. He escorted her to the car, holding her just in case she did pass out. These few moments were the only gentle moments Clark shared with Arial during the entire horrific event.

Clark and Arial were the last ones to leave the graveside, she had very little strength left, she had eaten scarcely anything, nor had she had a full night's sleep in several days. The walk from the graveside to the car was almost more than Arial could handle. Clark's assistance was invaluable. Arial did not want to leave Tara alone, she was imagining all the disgusting things that Tara would hear or imagine. Tara was petrified of rats and bugs, Arial's anxiety was heightened at the very thought of Tara hearing the dirt being shoveled onto the casket, she knew Tara would hear each shovel plummeting the dirt on top of her. Tara's fear of rats and bugs had been a life long phobia, that she had always failed to deal with. Arial's brain was so confused she could see the bugs and maggots slithering all through Tara's body.

Clark and Arial returned home, she knew she would return to the cemetery later, after the disguise of that horrendous hole was removed. Arial wanted to retrieve as many yellow buds as possible, she desperately wanted to dry the flowers and have a floral arrangement to set on her desk. She had to research this craft but she finally conquered the task. She hung the flowers upside down in a dark closet, so they would dry, but this took several months.

# Chapter Fourteen

## Horrible Information

After the funeral passed Arial was very aggravated, she had not heard one word from law enforcement. Arial felt that they should have contacted someone in the family, it did not matter who, just someone. This never occurred; this only caused Arial to be consumed with rage daily. She called her brothers to ask if they had any desire to attend a meeting with the District Attorney. Of course, they did not understand why; but they agreed to go with her. Arial scheduled the appointment at a time when each of them could attend. The appointment was scheduled with an Assistant District Attorney. His name was Mr. Ricer, a very nice man with very bad news. When Arial and her brother's arrived they were in for a loathing surprise. Mr. Ricer seemed to have no empathy whatsoever. He was so direct and to the point, it caused tears to flow freely from Arial and her brothers.

Arial and her brother's explained that they were not out for revenge, they knew that Don was very sick mentally, but they needed to be informed of the proceedings that were taking place. The explanation to Mr. Ricer was satisfactory, so the horrid events, he began to explain. Don, Tara's husband had stabbed her forty times with a hunting knife. Arial started to cry, her brother's mouths dropped wide open! Forty times! This was an over kill! Arial's head was spinning, what could Tara have possibly done to deserve one stab; much less forty! Don loved Tara very much, forty stabs could only mean an immense rage and hate; but this could not be possible. When Don was at his lowest point of the most severe depression; he would never have hurt Tara. This was a nightmare no one could have ever imagined!

Mr. Ricer informed Arial and her brothers that Don had been charged with homicide, or 1st degree murder. Don, at the present time was being evaluated to determine if he was competent to stand trial. Competent meant understanding right from wrong, if he completely understood what he did was wrong; and if he would be capable of assisting with his defense. Arial absolutely realized how sick Don actually was, the competency evaluations deeply concerned her. The benefit of doubt Arial had given Don initially was dwindling quickly. When they entered the District Attorney's office Arial's demeanor was calmer, but now she was outraged to the point that she could have killed Don if he had entered the door!

Arial's brother's explained that they loved Tara but Arial and Tara were extremely close, with this information Mr. Ricer decided that he would converse with Arial only. He assured each of them that he would inform Arial before the next hearing or if he received any new information concerning the case. Arial was satisfied for the moment, but that satisfaction did not last long. Arial had always been a very anxious, hyper woman. She wanted the answers yesterday; not tomorrow. This time, like so many others, the answers would be slower than ever.

A few days or maybe a week later the phone rang; it was Mr. Ricer, the District Attorney, the conversation began with Mr. Ricer asking how Arial was feeling, and of course Arial lied; she said she was fine. Then he began to explain what was occurring concerning the case. The next hearing had been scheduled, he informed Arial of the date and time; at this hearing the judge would determine if Don was competent to stand trial. Arial understood and planned to inform her brother's.

Arial asked the District Attorney if he had heard anything else concerning Don. He explained that he had received some information related to the initial interview, but he did not want to discuss the details on the phone. He had not talked to Don, but he would schedule an appointment for Arial to come in to discuss the details. She accepted that, wrote down the appointment time for the hearing and for her meeting with Mr. Ricer. Arial was always on the defensive, but she thanked him as cordially as possible. Mr. Ricer did not know Arial at all; when he made the decision to talk only with Arial, he had no idea what kind of developing situation he was creating. Arial would become a thorn in his side that he could not remove, a thorn that would cause so much aggravation and anxiety, Arial would become difficult to deal with.

Arial tried to wait patiently for the meeting with Mr. Ricer, it was only a few days; but it seemed like forever. The appointment finally arrived, Arial dreaded going but she needed to know anything she could discover. Mr. Ricer met at the door, she sat and of course there were the normal formalities; how are you doing, and so on. Then he began to fill Arial's brain with the horrible truths. Mr. Ricer had not spoken to Don personally, he was reviewing the initial interview that was transcribed the morning Don was arrested.

According to the interview, Don was very incoherent at times, he cried most of the time, he was covered with blood, he had not been allowed to clean up. According to the transcripts, Don used all the strength he could gather not to wake Tara up. His physical and mental condition was so severe; she had given him strict instructions not to wake her. He was pacing constantly, back and forth throughout the house, he thought he would explode if he could not speak to Tara, he had not forgotten her warning; and he took this warning very seriously. He postponed waking

Tara until he had lost all control. Don opened the bedroom door, Tara was sound asleep, and there was a sense of dread came over Don's body. If Don woke Tara he knew precisely how outraged she would be, he did not want this to occur, but it was as if he had lost all human control.

He proceeded toward the bed with caution; he never knew what type of reaction she would present, even in his fragile state of mind this concerned him.

Don could not take the loneliness or the quietness of the house any longer, he urgently needed to talk to Tara! He began to rub her shoulder and speak softly; hoping this would soften the decision to wake her. Unfortunately, this decision proved to be futile. Tara's reaction to Don waking her was more than Don could have ever imagined. She jumped from the bed, cursing him, calling him every son-of-a-bitch there was on the earth! According to the first interview, there was a hammer lying within Tara's grasp; she was hitting Don with her fist and then she seized the hammer and proceeded to try to hit Don with the hammer. Later Don recanted the statement concerning the hammer.

Tara was screaming, fighting, and cussing Don, if only Tara had not been so vicious she might be alive today. Don's state of mind was in a place that it had never been before. A place that totally took over his entire being, a place that would completely destroy his life and the lives of so many other people.

Don explained in the interview that he remembered reaching for the knife that hung on the wall, Tara was so infuriated she was almost delusional, she was ranting as she was trying to reach the bathroom; when she turned her back to Don she never would have ever imagined in her life the events that followed immediately.

Don stated that he seemed to be in a fog; a dream like illusion, not fully aware of what he doing, this was not planned; this was a freak act of human nature. Apparently, the first stab that Don delivered was to Tara's back, this first stab was forceful enough to compel Tara to fall to the floor. Don's constraint was completely withered, gone and he would not regain that constraint; at least not that night. He continued to stab Tara as she begged and cried for him to stop! Some way Tara managed to fight enough to turn on her back, Don was sitting on her, he continued his tirade; Tara did everything she could to defend herself, she had defense wounds on her hands and arms. Tara's attempted defense was useless; Don was a very strong man, he had full control over her. He continued to stab Tara; there were stab wounds in her head, chest, back, arms and abdomen. The fatal stab was to her chest.

Don was very emotional during this interview, he said the last words Tara spoke was, "I STILL LOVE YOU DON".

Don's body and brain had completely lost touch with any form of reality, no one knows how lengthy Don's rampage was, maybe he became tired or Tara ceased to move. According to the detectives, as Don described his actions; at the time there seemed to be no remorse. The crime scene photos and notes indicated that after Tara passed, Don apparently stood and proceeded to the bathroom, to reach the bathroom, Don had to step over Tara's lifeless body. Tara's body lay in a pool of blood, Don was covered with his wife's blood, but apparently; he nonchalantly, with no apparent concern stepped over her body, as if nothing had occurred. The evidence showed Don's bloody footprints leading away from Tara's body to the bathroom sink. He continued to hold the knife as he stood at the sink. The blood slowly dripped from his clothes and dripped in and on the sink, then continued to the floor. There was a large volume of blood on Don, so much so; it penetrated the linoleum flooring and descended into the plywood sub-floor. Why Don stood at the sink so long has never been determined, his hand prints were on the sink, almost as if he was using it for stability. At some point Don used a towel and attempted to wipe the blood from the knife blade, then he placed the towel and knife on the edge of the bathtub.

The brain is a magnificent organ, it controls the entire body, but when the functions of the brain decreases the body has no control. Don was like a walking zombie, no feelings, no comprehension of the magnitude of his actions. He was tired and sleepy, he stepped over Tara's body as he exited the bathroom. He lay on the bed and went to sleep. The crime scene photos revealed where he lay, there was a void around his body, there was blood only where his body lay. The length of time Don slept was never known or at least revealed.

Sometime after 1:00 A.M., Tony, Tara's youngest son returned home, the house was dark and quite, his parents' bedroom door was closed; which was normal, so Tony went directly to bed. Tony later remarked that the only sound he heard after he retired was a door closing. He was tired and he fell asleep quickly. Tony's room was located on the opposite end of the house from his parents room, but this house was a double wide mobile home, noise of any magnitude could probably be heard from any area in the house. Tony heard nothing but a closing of a door.

Somewhere in the time vicinity of 3:00 A.M., Tony felt something pushing him and calling his name, the light had been turned on; his eyes were having a difficult time adjusting to the light. The voice continued to call his name, instructing him to wake up; something was wrong with his mother, finally he realized it was his dad. Don, his dad, was desperately calling Tony's name, Tara would not wake up! Tony rolled over and there was his dad covered with blood, Tony screamed, "what have you done?" Tony jumped from the bed, pushed his dad aside, and ran to their bedroom! What Tony discovered would change his life forever.

Tara lay face up on the floor, covered with blood and laying in a pool of blood, Tony went directly to his mother's side and tried to wake her; with no success. He tried to find a pulse, there was none; he could feel the coolness of her body, he knew she was dead! He quickly called 911;

he was screaming to the operator that his dad killed his mother! Then he heard a noise, he jumped from extreme fright; there was his dad walking toward him, this petrified Tony, he dropped the phone and ran from the house, as he ran he turned and glanced behind him, his dad appeared to be chasing him. This terrified Tony even more, he did not have a clue why his dad was chasing him, but he was terrified that his dad might be trying to seize him to hurt him also.

Tony was still running, when suddenly he heard sirens and he saw flashing lights, He was scared almost to death, but he began waving at the police car, they slowed to a crawl; Tony began screaming that his dad was chasing him, and that his mother was dead! The police stared straight ahead into the darkness, suddenly a silhouette began to appear beyond the bright headlights, it was Don; covered with blood. The police instructed Tony to quickly get into the back seat of their car! Police cars continued to arrive, the next one quickly stopped and handcuffed Don and placed him in another police car! Tony had to remain in the police car, he had to be interviewed, and he did not care, he was so scared but he worried about his mother, he knew she was dead; he was thinking about all the pain she had to endure at the hands of his dad. He knew her fear had been much greater than his, and he loved his mother more than any other person in his life. Tony desperately wanted to escape the back seat of that car, he wanted to be with his sister and brother, his anxiety level increased as time seemed to be prolonged, finally; after what seemed to be hours, the police allowed him to return to his family.

Tony's life changed that night; depression seemed to control his body. To this day, Tony says the first thing he sees when he opens his eyes every morning is his mother lying dead in a pool of blood, and the last vision he has at night is exactly the same. Sometimes there is very little sleep, some nights are better than others. Tony's days are not much better, he is on medications for depression and anxiety; he also has had extensive therapy. The family hopes that someday his condition will improve, but it is doubtful, to discover his mother's body dead and to realize that his dad perpetrated this horrendous act would be more than most people could overcome.

# Chapter Fifteen

## Don's Hearing

Arial was satisfied but madder than hell with this information! Mr. Ricer informed her of all the information he had knowledge of and explained that he would call her as he received more information. Arial left, she was extremely aggravated; at this time she did not believe that Tara had tried to hit Don with a hammer. Don was a perfectionist when it pertained to his tools. There was a place for everything and he demanded that each tool be returned to its place immediately after its use. There was no way that a hammer would be left in the bedroom, this absolutely would not be allowed. This was driving Arial crazy; she was determined to uncover the truth, how; she was not sure. As she drove home her thoughts were everywhere, never remaining on any one particular thought long enough to be decisive, she was confused, mad, her sister was dead, and she did not know how to deal with that fact.

Rumors began to roam, people were saying things, some were true, and some were not, but Arial's strong will was unwavering, somehow she thought that she could unravel this mess by herself. There was a problem; Arial's mental status was not top-notch at this time, she cried daily, the lack of food was beginning to show, she was eating but not enough. She had lost more than ten pounds and this was only the beginning. She was trying to work, with very little sleep, her mind and body felt as if it was running at full speed, but her brain simply could not function as well as it had before all this mess.

One rumor, which was a fact; Don had called home from the jail and left a message on the answering machine. The message implied that Don was not aware of anything that had occurred. His message was for Tara, it said that the joke was over, Tara had better get him out of jail, enough was enough! It was not funny anymore! This was totally ridiculous, did he not remember, had his brain totally blocked out everything? There was always the possibility that he was trying to scam everybody into thinking that he was crazy; could he possibly be thinking this could be a way to get away with murder? Of course Arial's brain was doing flip flops concerning this possibility, could Don be released; totally free if they thought he was crazy?

The day finally arrived for the hearing, the judge would determine if Don was competent to stand trial. Arial was so determined to make sure that Don saw her in the courtroom. Arial's mother managed to acquire enough strength to accompany her children to the hearing. There were two sides, one for the defense and one side for the prosecution. Don's family sat on the defense side; while Tara's family sat on the prosecution's side. Arial began gazing for the most appropriate location, a seat where she could see Don and where she would also be visible to him. She wanted him to see the expressions on her face, she wanted him to understand just how much she hated him for destroying her life. Arial was aware that Tara's death had destroyed two families but she truly felt that it had did more damage to her than to anyone else. These words she never spoke out loud, but at the time she sincerely believed this. Arial honestly thought that no one could be suffering more than she, not even Tara's children. Arial was so mistaken, her depression was so severe, her thoughts mostly consisted of herself, her loss, grief, sorrow and pain.

The judge entered the courtroom, everyone stood as he entered and plopped into his big chair, then they were allowed to sit. The normal formalities followed, the defense and the prosecution had a few words to speak, then two psychiatrist, one for the defense and one for the prosecution took the stand. They both concluded that Don had major mental issues but he knew right from wrong, he was aware of the crime he had committed, and he was mentally stable; enough to aid in his defense. The judge then spoke to Don; asking him if he understood everything concerning the hearing. Don replied yes. The judge then explained to Don that he was charged with first-degree murder, without bail. The judge explained to Don that he would be detained at the county jail until the trial date, which had not been set.

During this time, Arial closely watched Don's every movement, he was very aware of Arial's presence, at times Don would cautiously turn his head toward Arial, each time he saw that she was staring at him. He would quickly turn his head toward the front of the courtroom. Don's appearance was not good; he wore an orange jumpsuit furnished by the jail, when he entered he was handcuffed and his legs were shackled. Arial did not have any compassion for Don at all. She would not have cared if he had been wrapped in chains, this was the man that had killed her sister, at that moment she would not have cared if he had dropped dead on the spot, silently she wished he would. Arial's deepest desire was for Don to suffer immensely, in the same manner Tara had suffered, but she did realize that would never occur.

The hearing was very short, Arial heard what she needed to hear, and Don would be locked up until his trial date. Don's family was not happy, he was sick, they prayed he would receive the care he so desperately needed in jail, but they had their reservations. Arial also knew that Don was very sick, but he had killed her sister, Tara. Arial would never be able to forgive him, and she would never forget.

# Chapter Sixteen

## Depression

Arial had returned to work weeks before the last hearing, she was allowed only three days for funeral leave, she needed six months; but she returned as required. Arial's return to work did not go well; she was so anxious and depressed she could not concentrate. The paperwork was a nightmare, she stared at the pencil in her hand, and the papers, she knew she had to write something on the paper but, God; she did not know what. She was so confused, lost; almost as if she had never done these things. She stared at the machinery that she at one time could operate proficiently, but now; she was not sure. She had a partner, her name was Mary, and she was also a good friend. Arial went to her almost in tears; she explained that she absolutely could not even comprehend the paperwork. Mary felt so sorry for Arial, she helped Arial with every issue concerning the job. This became an everyday occurrence, Arial's eyes peered at the paperwork each day, it appeared to be a bunch of mumble jumble, she watched the machinery, she tried to operate the machinery, but she had lost that small nitch that she needed to perform the job correctly. Arial would get so upset she would begin to cry. Mary, her friend; always came to her rescue, if not for Mary, Arial may have lost her job. Slowly, after a few weeks, Arial began to regain some control, her performance on the job was not perfect, but at least she required less help.

One day at work, everyone was on break, the plant nurse came through the door and announced that Mary had five minutes to get to the nurses' station for a random drug test. Arial panicked, she was still taking the anti-anxiety drugs that her aunt had given her, and she did not have a prescription for them. If her name was picked, she knew it would show in her urine. She needed her job, not only for monetary value, but also to help keep her sane. She was fortunate that day, but as soon as she returned home, she called the doctor to make an appointment. Arial went the next day, she dreaded seeing the doctor; she would have to rehash the entire ordeal, even then the doctor might not give her a prescription. Arial was correct, she had to explain the entire scenario; from start to finish. This was very upsetting for Arial, and the doctor could see her anxiousness and depression. She explained about her job, the doctor listened very intently and he watched her carefully. Her blood pressure was high, especially for Arial; her blood pressure was always low. The doctor decided that Arial needed the anxiety medicines plus she needed an anti-depressant. Arial frowned concerning the anti-depressant, she had only heard bad things about that kind of medicine. The doctor was adamant, Arial needed both; not just one. Arial finally agreed, she had to have the prescriptions. She was very frightened about the ant-depressant, she had heard horrible things that people had done while taking these medications. She went to the pharmacy, she wondered what the pharmacist would think about her having to take these medicines. Would he think she was crazy, did it mean she was crazy? Most of the time she felt like she needed to be stored away in a place with the insane, she thought that she would fit in very well. Arial knew her thoughts and feelings were not normal but she did not care, she was consumed with quilt because she was alive and Tara was buried in a dark hole and God only knew what was crawling in and out of her body. Arial would have freely exchanged places with Tara; Tara was so young, seven years younger than Arial.

Arial returned to work feeling safe concerning the drug tests. The anti-depressants were not making her feel any better, her job performance was poor at best, her daily life sucked. A few weeks later she had to return to the doctor to be evaluated concerning the medicines. There was no improvement; her moods remained the same, her activity level was virtually nil, and she cried so much. The doctor decided to change the medicine, she was to return in three weeks. This process continued for two years with no improvement.

During this two year time span Arial wanted to just go away, each night as she filled the tub with water; she watched it slowly rise by the inch. She wanted to slip in and relax to the point of sliding downward into the water, float away and never see the light of day ever again. She knew her pain would disappear, she thought she would be happy and she would definitely see Tara again. This was a nightly ritual, she wondered if it would hurt to be without air. She kept these thoughts to herself, she did not have any desire to speak to anyone, not anyone but her sister.

The legal aspects of the case continued against Don. Local or area doctors determined that he was competent to stand trial for murder. Suddenly, the defense asked the judge to allow Don to be sent to the state hospital in Crowleigh to be evaluated by more professional and experienced doctors, so of course in the name of justice; he agreed. Arial sat in her seat, deeply disturbed by this interruption and wondered where was the justice for her sister? Arial assumed that Don would be sent to Crowleigh hospital immediately, she was thrilled simply to know that he would not be in town for a while. A few weeks passed and Arial heard from someone that Don remained in town. Outrage began to escalate, she thought she would explode, she called the D.A,s office, of course he was in court, she had to leave a voice message. The only words she spoke were, “why is he still hear?” The tone of her voice was overbearing and defiant. Then Arial slammed the phone down and waited. Later in the day, the phone rang; it was Mr. Ricer. There were no hello’s, how are you’s, just; “the reason he is still here is because, these things take time!” There was an instant echo in Arial’s ear, he had slammed the phone down very vigorously, she knew he was ticked off at her, but she did not care. Arial almost found some humor in his response, but there was only one thing, Don was still in town! She wanted Don gone, preferably from the face of the earth, but out of town would be sufficient for the moment.

A week or more passed, Arial let Mr. Ricer’s ears rest, but there was a limit, and that limit had ran out. The self-control she labored so hard with had completely diminished. She wanted information, so she made that desperate phone call, Mr. Ricer answered, Arial was determined to be cordial; she was terrified that he would discontinue any further communication with her. She knew he was not required to share legal information, he was doing it as a common courtesy, and she did appreciate it. She apologized for her sarcasm, and he instantly explained that Don had been taken to Crowleigh Hospital. He continued to explain that Don may be gone for at least a month, maybe longer. Arial thanked him sincerely and hung up. Calmness seemed to flow throughout Arial’s body, a feeling of relief consumed her. Why? She did not understand, she simply felt better.

Arial’s life crept along each day, she went to work, or at least her body was present; her mind, well it was somewhere. The thoughts in Arial’s brain changed by the second, even at this time she still worried about Tara laying underground in the dirt. It was getting cold, Tara did not like cold weather, she loved the sunshine beaming on her face and the wind slightly blowing her long curly hair. She enjoyed the outdoors; swinging in the swing that Don had made for her and their grandchildren. These precious moments that Tara cherished so much were gone, her grandchildren missed her terribly, but they remembered the special times they shared with their grandmother.

One particular night Arial was working the second shift, when she exited the plant, it was cold, the wind was blowing very strong and it was raining cats and dogs; so to speak. Arial's car was parked quite a distance from the entrance, she did not have an umbrella, this meant she had to run. She was soaked by the time she reached her car. She cranked her car, and sat there staring into the darkness; she did not want to go home, there was only an empty house there. Clark was there, but he did not matter, his presence was only an annoyance, there was one pleasant thought, Clark would be asleep. Arial had not loved Clark as a husband for many years, she remained married to him to assure herself that her children would have a better childhood. It was still raining, Arial had no idea how long she had been sitting there, but she knew she had to go home, reluctantly she drove from the parking lot. She was about half way home, and the tears began to flow, she was deeply concerned about Tara, it was cold and raining; was the water seeping in and around Tara's body, she could not remove these images from her mind, she could almost feel Tara's fear. Tara was alone, no one to comfort her, was she cold, could she possibly be wet? Arial cried uncontrollably the entire distance home. It was truly a miracle that Arial did not have an accident, the rain appeared to be falling from the sky in sheets and tears were streaming from Arial's eyes, she could barely see the road. Arial's grief was going to destroy her if she did not get some form of positive, professional help.

Arial visited Tara's grave daily, she would just sit there and talk to her, and she knew that she would not receive a response. There were times Arial would sit and cry for an hour or more, she believed that Tara was aware that she was present, and she was sure that Tara wanted her there. Arial began a quest of sorts; each holiday, and the relevance of the holiday to Tara's death did not matter. Arial would purchase a card, write a simple note inside and laminate the card to protect it from the elements. She would purchase a fresh floral arrangement, place the card appropriately and arrange it in the vase. Arial did this for each holiday in the year, Christmas, Veteran's Day, Easter, Valentine's Day, Tara's birthday, any and all holidays were included. Once she went to visit Tara's grave and someone had placed a floral arrangement in the vase that Arial did not approve of; she became upset and discarded the ugly flowers. She replaced them with what she considered appropriate, then she informed the family; including Tara's children that she would assume the responsibility of caring for Tara's gravesite. Of course, everyone agreed to let Arial have this responsibility. Arial continued this tradition for quite a few years, Don's headstone was already in place beside Tara's, Arial would clean the grass and debris from Tara's headstone and place it on Don's. She despised the idea that he would be buried beside Tara. No one knew what Arial hoped to accomplish by wreaking havoc on Don's headstone, but maybe it made her feel better, who knows; what she really craved was to locate a sledge hammer and burst it into a million pieces. Arial could envision the cement slowly breaking and pieces scattering on the green grass and the wind blustering and scattering the remaining mess out of sight.

Shortly after Tara passed Arial purchased two plots beside Tara; for Clark and herself. Arial had no thoughts concerning how dramatically her life would change within just a few short years. Arial's attitude and actions had risen to a level of gigantic proportions, the sweet, kind, caring person, the lady that had always did what she was told, never questioned anything; that lady had disappeared. Arial had always smiled, she appeared to be happy at all times, but now the glow in her cheeks had disappeared, the sadness seemed to scream from her eyes, the rage escaped from her lips. This was the new Arial; and it would be a long time before signs of recovery would be seen.

Don was in the state mental hospital for more than a month, Arial did not care, she did want this nightmare over, but at least Don was away from everyone. A problem did remain, Tara was gone, and no one could get their crap together, especially Arial. She was dead and Don had killed her, so it really did not matter where Don was at; this important fact was what controlled the families thoughts. Don had taken her away from their lives, everyone thought of her daily; but they also had very vivid thoughts concerning Don. Arial's four brothers would have killed him instantly if the opportunity had presented itself.

Tara's children were in extreme mental anguish. Lela, Tara's daughter exhibited the most visible signs. After about six weeks she finally returned to work, but her skills as a sales person had quickly diminished, the expert persona she exhibited on the phone talking to people in the USA and other countries had almost disappeared. It was also being noticed by the clients, but as each client realized the reason, they showed sympathy and more patience. She would become so nauseated she would vomit in her office trash can. Lela was lucky; she had great employers that allowed her as much time as possible to return to her normal self. Lela never completely recovered, but she improved with medication and time. She had two brothers, Tony the youngest, who discovered his mother's body, is on permanent disability because of anxiety and depression, he also has seizures. The doctors are not sure if the seizures are related to his mother's death or numerous other reasons. Tara's middle son has been on drugs and alcohol, lost custody of his children and jobless at times. Tara would be so proud to know that he completely reversed his life. He is working, he regained custody of his four children, and is completely off drugs. All of Tara's children, her most prized accomplishments; have with time made a remarkable recovery.

# Chapter Seventeen

## Call to the White House

The days passed slowly for Arial while Don was in the state hospital, she did not want him to return, but she wanted the entire ordeal over. She actually wanted him hung from the court square in the midst of the world. But even as screwed up as her brain was she was well aware that would never happen. Arial's brothers and she would be shocked at the final outcome. Don finally returned from the state hospital after several months. Mr. Ricer called Arial and informed her of his return, a hearing had been scheduled for the judge to determine if Don was truly competent to stand trial. Arial expressed her concern to Mr. Ricer of the possibility that he would be declared not competent, he tried to reassure her the only way he knew how; and that was not to worry so much. That was like speaking to a brick wall, Arial's optimism had disappeared, pessimism had taken full control of Arial. This caused anger beyond her control, the medications Arial was taking; not one was aiding to a recovery. She was a delusional mess, she would sit in her kitchen alone, drinking mass amounts of coffee and smoking triple the cigarettes that was normal for her. She would stare from her kitchen window, there was a garden center at the end of the street, she had a full view of all the flowers and trees. Before Arial's world began tumbling down all around her, she would have been purchasing the flowers and trees. She loved the outdoors, but now the desire for the beauty of the flowers had dissipated. The desire to enjoy life, the outdoors, sunshine and even cloudy rainy days were gone. Now she would remain in the house, very seldom dressing, she never accomplished anything, she certainly did not clean the house anymore, she did not care about anything in life. Arial's thoughts were totally about Tara, and how to make sure that Don paid with his life. Arial's job was one way she maintained her sanity. Arial left her safe house only when absolutely necessary.

The hearing date had arrived; there was no reason for Arial to attend, but heaven or hell could keep her away. The hearing was very short, the overweight judge entered, and every one had to stand as he entered, why, Arial did not understand. In Arial's opinion he was no better than anyone else, just a man that held a gavel he could pound to gain control and composure in what he considered his court room. The defense and the prosecution called their expert witnesses, each stating their professional opinions that Don was competent to stand trial. The doctors agreed that Don did have very serious mental disorders, but each agreed that he understood the difference between right and wrong and that he was mentally competent to aid in his defense. The judge listened intently to each doctor; he sat quietly in his big chair as he was reviewing documents. He then began to speak directly to Don, he asked Don if he understood the proceedings, Don spoke very quietly that he did understand and that he was aware of the consequences of a jury trial. The judge studied Don's facial expressions and body language, his voice tone, he was searching for any slight detail that would show that he did not understand, Don revealed only positive reactions. The judge seemed to be satisfied, he only required a moment to schedule a trial date. The trial was scheduled for months away, the justice system was so back logged, the trial would have to wait it's turn. Don would be detained to the county satellite jail until his trial date. Court was dismissed; Don was lead out by officers of the court. The walk for Don was slow, he was handcuffed and shackles connected his ankles, he turned and stared at his family, his parents were in tears. Arial was not family any longer, but she did receive a glimpse from Don; a very sad and solemn look, almost as if asking for forgiveness. There would never be forgiveness from Arial, or her brother's.

Arial returned home concerned about a jury trial, no one knew what the outcome of a jury would be. Arial continued to concentrate about the fact that Don was released before the seventy-two hour requirement. If Don had not been released early, maybe, just maybe Tara would still be alive. Arial wanted this investigated, and if possible; laws should be changed. She realized that the laws concerning mental illness were created by each individual state. Arial's mental stability could be questioned, she was not at her best. She became obsessed with the idea that she could possibly draw attention to this issue that desperately needed to be addressed. She had no knowledge of the states branches of government, and the only place she could think of to call was the White House. She had no idea how easy it would be to acquire the information she desired. She placed a call to 411 and asked for the phone number of the White House, it was given to her without any questions. She placed the call and immediately the phone was answered, she asked for the names of each member of each branch of government in the state of South Carolina. The lady that answered the phone at the White House was so polite and nice, she replied that she would gladly provide the information that Arial had requested. The lady asked for Arial's full name, address, state and zip code. She then said that the information would be sent shortly. Arial assumed that she would be placed on a watch list, but she did not care, she wanted desperately to make an attempt at having the laws changed. A few days passed and a large manila envelope arrived from the White House. Arial was astonished at how quickly it arrived, she was also thrilled that she had something that had come directly from the White House.

She immediately opened the envelope, and she was even more pleasantly surprised. The information concerning each member was overwhelming, their personal home address was listed, personal cell numbers, office numbers, e-mail addresses, and wife's names. Arial was truly amazed at the amount of information that was released concerning government officials. She thought this was eerie, for Arial the information would be used to suggest that the appropriate officials at least consider reviewing the laws concerning admittance into state mental facilities. She also realized that there were a lot of people in this crazy mixed up world that would want this information for ulterior motives. This was not Arial, she just wanted something positive, if possible to emanate from the death of her sister Tara.

Arial tried to think of a direct approach, a written letter, phone call, or something, she was not sure. She placed a call to the Domestic Violence office, she explained everything, from start to finish; she explained what her goal was, but she was not quite sure how to get started. Arial was asked to come into their office the next day, and of course Arial agreed. She always got upset when she had to start from the beginning and explain the entire ordeal, and she knew this would be asked. Arial arrived at the office the next day very apprehensive. She had taken her medications, she wanted to appear as if she had some sense left. The lady could see straight through Arial, it seemed that no amount of medication could hide the intense depression that revealed itself on Arial's face. The lady was very patient with Arial; she allowed her all the time Arial needed to progress through the painful experience. After all was said and done, the caring lady explained where to begin. She explained to Arial that a handwritten letter to each person would be best. The letter would seem to be more personal if hand-written. Arial should explain the circumstances in a very personal manner. She should explain the great loss to her family and Tara's children. She should also call the members of the state offices, talk to them one on one, ask for their input or at least examine the laws pertaining to this particular case.

Arial began hand writing each letter, describing the horrific accounts that led to her sister; Tara's death. She included the grief and tremendous loss her family had and was still enduring. She almost begged for someone to examine the mental health laws in the state. Arial was very dedicated; she wrote each day until her hands could not write any longer. She would have to rest a day to allow her hands to recuperate. She stared at the list of names, there were so many, she had no idea how many politicians there were in the state government. Arial wondered if she would ever complete this mission, but she did prevail. Slowly she began to mail the letters, a few a day; until finally she completed all of them. A few weeks passed, Arial was wondering if she would ever receive a response, she had worked so hard, never left the house, this was her first priority at the moment. That moment transformed into weeks of relentless work, which she would gladly repeat if only she received any positive feedback. Some days she would gaze from her kitchen window, Autumn was beginning to show, the leaves were beginning to show their vibrant colors, the son was still bright, but she did not have time; or even had the desire to enjoy the slight cooler temperatures. She was waiting for the phone to ring, or the mail man to arrive with some acknowledgement that her letters had been read. Suddenly, out of the blue, she received a letter from one politician, who; she does not remember, it has been many years, some dates and names have been forgotten. The letter deeply expressed their sympathy for the families loss. He gave the impression that at some time he would expand his knowledge of the state mental laws, but for the present time he once again expressed his condolences. Arial did appreciate the thought but she wanted and needed a more aggressive response.

The days and weeks passed slowly and finally she began to receive phone calls and more letters, actually after a couple of months she had been contacted by each of the politicians. Unfortunately for Arial, none of the responses were very optimistic, each said they would inquire about the laws. She was extremely disappointed, so she began the mission once more, the second time she received fewer responses. Arial's thoughts were that, these terrible events did not happen to someone in their family, so they did not take it too seriously. If it had happened to someone in their family, their response would be exactly the opposite.

Arial's depression continued to worsen; she had not accomplished what she had set out to do, but it was not from the lack of determination. She was continuing to visit her doctor for follow-ups concerning her depression. This was her primary care doctor, and he did not have the expertise of a psychiatrist. Arial's next visit was not what she expected. He informed her that he could no longer prescribe depression medicine. He insisted she see a psychiatrist, she needed therapy, probably long term therapy. Arial did not care to hear this, she did not want to lay on a sofa and disclose all her inner thoughts, but she needed the correct medicines and she knew this. Arial's knowledge of this information did not change the fact, Tara was dead; Arial's life was not important any longer, she was consumed with guilt, Tara was dead and Arial was alive, it should have been the opposite. For some reason unknown to Arial; God had chosen Tara, and Arial did not understand. Tara was a gift to the world, maybe God had a plan for Tara in heaven that Arial was not yet qualified for. She did not know, Arial would talk out loud to Tara; she asked her if she was sitting with God on his pearly white throne. She frequently warned Tara about her unique vocabulary, she explained to Tara that she could not speak or even think those words in heaven, God had the ability to hear what she was thinking, she warned her to be careful. Tara always had a delightful sense of humor, Arial often asked Tara if she was giving God extra reasons to smile and laugh, Arial knew that God would enjoy having Tara in heaven.

# Chapter Eighteen

## Arial's Need for a Psychiatrist

Arial's doctor made the appointment with the psychiatrist, she definitely did not want to go but her medicine was running out, she had to go. She had about a month to think about it, but at that moment she was not sure that she would go. She told Clark, her husband that she was not sure if she was going, he stared at her with such conviction and instructed her sternly that she had better go. This ticked Arial off, he had never allowed her to express her feelings or thoughts to him, he would say; I do not want to talk about it. He would walk away and leave her standing there alone and so depressed. Arial's love for Clark had dwindled years ago, resentment had become very harsh towards Clark, and she did not care. Tara's death had damaged Arial's mental health to the point that life was not important anymore, if only she could live long enough to be assured that Don would pay severely for the horrible act he had had inflicted on Tara, after that Arial did not care. She wanted to live just to see that he was suffering, she wanted him to suffer, and the later of the outcome would be his death.

Arial's daughter-in-law, Renee, was an inspiration for Arial, when Renee had the time she would listen to Arial. Renee was close to Tara, so these talks would upset Renee to the point of tears, Arial mentioned to Renee that she might not see the psychiatrist, Renee revealed her shock, not just verbally; but the expression that loomed from her face was fear! Renee did recover from the shock of the words Arial had spoken. Renee regained her composure enough to insist that Arial to see the psychiatrist. Renee tried to explain to Arial that she was not the same person, she could see the depression on Arial's face. The words that escaped from Arial's lips were not normal in in any way. Renee also expressed to Arial that her normal everyday actions had disappeared. Arial did not smile, or talk with any sense, she rambled from one thought to another without completing a viable sentence. Arial listened to Renee, Renee was her first daughter-in-law, and Arial loved her like a second daughter. She knew that Renee would not lie or exaggerate her actions, she was portraying the anxious and depressed Arial as she truly appeared to her.

Renee's intervention helped Arial make a definite decision to talk to the psychiatrist. The appointment was very close, Arial still did not want to talk to a quack, but she remembered the words that Renee had spoken to her, she wondered if Renee thought that she was crazy. Arial was well aware that she had many problems, the day finally arrived for her appointment with the psychiatrist, she went; dreading this with a passion. The doctor's office was out of town, she went alone, and she was very nervous. She arrived early and that was good, she had a million questions to answer on a clip board. Arial had a problem with the questions, her brain was very screwed up, it did not think or comprehend most of the questions, most she left blank. Shortly the nurse called her name, clip board in hand, she proceeded to the doctor's office. The door was closed behind her, she sat in a very uncomfortable chair. Arial began to investigate the room, there was that couch, she would refuse to lay on that thing. There were documents hanging on the walls, these documents were to show patients that he had several degrees, where he graduated from and where he did his internships. They were very impressive, the colleges were well known and reputable. This information was also to make the patients think that he was capable of helping them through tragic events in their lives that had totally obliterated their brains. It worked, Arial did feel more secure. The doctor had a huge expensive desk, quite elaborate actually, Arial knew without question that he made a lot of money. Arial did not have any money, if not for insurance she would not be there. She had scanned the entire room before he entered, she was wondering if there was a video camera in the room, a way to view her reactions, she really did not care, she wished he would hurry up!

The door handle turned, the slight noise startled her, and it had been so quite in the room. The doctor introduced himself; he already knew who she was, and a few things about her. He began by asking about her family, just as a courtesy; she assumed. A few moments of casual conversations then he asked that she start from the beginning, Arial knew she would have to talk about everything; from beginning to end. She began by explaining how close Tara and she had been and the occurrences that led to her death. Of course she cried, he could see the depression and the anxiety, but he needed her to talk about all the details, he heard the strain in her voice, the uncertainty in her body language, from all of these details he learned a great deal about how seriously sick Arial was. The session was to last only an hour, he now needed to talk to her about prescribing medications. He started with an anti-depressant, he chose Prozac, Arial was terrified of that word, she had heard horrible stories about things people had done while taking this drug. She quickly informed him that she did not want to take Prozac, and she explained why! The doctor quickly explained that it was the most widely prescribed anti-depressant in the world and produced very good results. This did not convince Arial, the thought of that drug scared her beyond her imagination. The doctor was adamant about the drug. He began to explain a couple of side effects related to the drug. The one that really set Arial off was the fact that it would probably diminish her sex drive significantly. Well, Arial sprang from her chair to the middle of the floor and then leaned toward his desk. Arial screamed to the doctor, her sister was dead and he was concerned about her sex drive, she continued to scream that she was forty seven years old and that she could care less if she never had sex again as long as she lived! The doctor had pushed his chair backwards, not knowing what Arial's next reaction would be! She had startled him, he was not expecting that rage of anger; an explosion of frustration that had been building inside her for almost two years. What he did not realize was that explosion had been steaming within her for almost her entire life, but he would never be privy to that information.

Arial finally calmed down, and returned to her chair, the doctor slowly pushed his chair close to his desk. He then began to speak again, he began to instruct her how and when to take the anti-depressant, Arial was much calmer by then, she listened intently. She was frightened; she certainly did not want to take the medicine incorrectly. The session ended and a further appointment was made for a month.

Arial checked out with her prescription and statement, she hurried to her car; she knew she had lost control, she did not care, she just wanted to go home. She sat in the car for a moment, she stared at the prescription; God, she did not want to take that medicine, then she read the statement, he had hand-written the diagnosis; severe major depression. Arial stared at the diagnosis, was she really that bad? She knew her brain was screwed up, but not to that degree.

She drove home, a little more concerned than before, she felt so much guilt, Tara was dead and she was still alive, that bothered her so much. The intense guilt and the longing for Tara to return caused Arial not to care if she ever recovered. Arial, on a daily basis wanted to die, she had no reason to live, or at least that is what she believed. The fact remained that she did not have the guts to take her own life, which in the end was a good thing.

# Chapter Nineteen

## Possibility of a Dismissal

Arial called the District Attorney and asked if she could see him, just to find out what was happening. Quickly and nicely, almost to quickly he said yes; she could come in the next day. At first, Arial did not think anything about his quick reply, she wanted to be updated. When she arrived, she noticed a distant facial expression, she wondered what was on his mind. He began to talk about Don and the fact that at his first interview he had made the statement that Tara had tried to hit him with a hammer, but later recanted the statement. Arial was aware of the statement but she did not believe that Tara had tried to hit Don with the hammer, and she made that crystal clear. The District Attorney was rumbling through the papers that lay on his desk, he was not looking at Arial, he was trying his best not to look at her. Suddenly a much unexpected remark seemed to echo in the room, Arial thought she had misunderstood, she asked him to repeat what he had just said. He looked at her then, he casually commented that he was considering dismissing the charges against Don. Arial was completely dumbfounded, she would have fallen from the chair from a soft breeze! She stared at him, she was listening but the only words she heard were dismissal. She became totally confused, so bewildered she rose from the chair and left the office. She managed to find her car, she sat there and cried for a few moments. The rage started to consume her body, she was so mad, she thought she might explode! She immediately went home and called her brother Steven. He was slow answering the phone, but when he finally did answer Arial was so distraught, between her crying and sobbing Steven could hardly understand a word she was speaking. He screamed at her to calm down, and stop crying. Arial slowed enough to inform Steven that there had been a discussion about dismissing the case! Steven was just as upset. Arial asked if he would accompany her to an appointment with the actual head District Attorney. Arial explained that as soon as she scheduled the appointment she would call him. She was so upset, she called the District Attorney's office and asked for an appointment with Mr. Straner, the head of the office. The receptionist quickly scheduled the appointment for the next day. Steven and Arial were early as usual, they sat down and waited their turn. Arial had a nervous habit, her legs were crossed and one leg was swinging as fast as possible. The majority of the time Arial was not conscious of the leg swinging, this was one of those times. The fear that Don could walk out of jail a free man was more than she could imagine.

Arial heard her name called, Steven and she followed the receptionist to Mr. Straner's office. Arial could see quickly that he was not thrilled to see them. The expression on his face showed aggravation and very little interest. Arial began to explain partially why they were there. He immediately interrupted her, saying they had to follow the law to the letter. Arial asked if that included dismissing the case against Don, she explained that Mr. Ricer suggested that could be a possibility. Mr. Staner defiantly replied no, there would not be a dismissal. He continued to explain that Mr. Ricer had very little experience with cases of this magnitude, and he assured them there would not be a dismissal. This news brought relief to Arial and Steven, they thanked Mr. Staner and left, he had definitely eased their mind.

Arial waited to call Mr. Ricer; she assumed that he was ticked off because she went above his authority to his superior, the head District Attorney; Mr. Staner. A week had passed before she made that dreaded phone call. She expected hostility, but that did not happen. The receptionist answered the phone, Arial asked for Mr. Ricer, she was informed that he was out of town; she said, you can leave a message, which Arial did. She only asked that he call her back. Arial did not believe for a minute that he was out of town, he was avoiding her, she was sure of that. That was okay, she would call again the next day. He had to answer the phone sooner or later, she could wait! Arial called for approximately two weeks, each call, she was informed that he was out of town. She began to wonder; he had never avoided her that long regarding anything. Arial hoped and prayed that she had not intimidated him to the point that he would refuse to share legal information with her. She had to know everything, Tara was her sister, Don had killed her and he had to pay. Arial honestly believed that her constant calling and badgering the District Attorney was aiding in the case, but it actually was not. She was aggravating everyone but she did not care, she was so determined to be totally involved with any and all aspects of the case; she would do or say anything to acquire information. What she did not realize was that they were not informing her of all of their discoveries. If only she could calm down and be rational, but for Arial that was not possible. If this disgusting episode in her life did not soon end, Arial would be headed straight to the looney bin!

A week later following her last phone call to the District Attorney, Arial was just about at the end of her last nerve! She rose that morning with intense anxiety before her feet hit the floor. It was too early to call the District Attorney's office, she sat quietly alone after Clark left for work. She was quite but her mind was racing, if he did not answer the phone this time she intended to go to his office. She knew he was there, regardless of what the receptionist said, she was sure that he had ordered the receptionist to lie and tell her he was not there! She had a couple of hours to wait before the office opened, it was barely breaking daylight, it was cloudy and misting rain. She went to the coffee maker to refill her cup, this was probably her fourth cup; the caffeine was not helping her anxiety. She gazed out the window, wishing the sun was shining, she wished it; but she also knew sun or no sun, it would not improve her attitude. She was mad, she needed to talk to Mr. Ricer, she was scared a decision would be made without her knowledge.

It was nine o'clock, finally; Arial hands were shaking, and she desperately needed Mr. Ricer to answer the phone, not his voice mail. She picked up the phone, she stood there for a moment, praying for the best. She was honestly frightened to push those buttons on the phone. Something inside her insisted she make the phone call. The phone began ringing and of course the receptionist answered, Arial asked for Mr. Ricer, thank God, she replied; "I will transfer you". Mr. Ricer answered, Arial was almost in shock. She immediately apologized for speaking with his supervisor, hoping that might soften the issue. Mr. Ricer explained that he had attended a seminar in California. He was so pleasant; he asked if she could come to his office, he had quite a few things to discuss with her. Arial immediately said yes, whenever was convenient for him. Mr. Ricer gave her an appointment for that afternoon, she was so elated, it had been so long since she had received any information. The elation caused more anxiety, she had no idea what he wanted to discuss with her. God, it was several hours before the appointment. She could not just sit there in the house and worry, she looked around the house, she decided that she should clean, it needed it. She would vacuum, and dust, anything to pass the time. She tried to work in the house, but she would find herself sitting down, with the vacuum beside her. Arial's mind was wandering with thoughts that had absolutely nothing to do with cleaning. She would make herself get off her buns, but she was constantly stopping.

She discontinued the vacuuming and decided to load the clothes washer. There were plenty of dirty clothes, and she knew that Clark would by-pass the washer, in fact Clark would by-pass anything if it represented work. Arial sorted the colored clothes; it seemed to take her forever, if only she would not stop and begin to think. Thinking was her downfall, her thoughts seemed to be different from anyone else's. Arial wanted things her way and was completely surprised when anyone did not agree with her. She honestly believed she was right and everyone else was wrong and this included the professionals. Arial had finally managed to waste enough time, and it was time to go to Mr. Ricer's office. She looked around the house and decided that she would clean the house thoroughly sooner or later.

Arial arrived early as usual, hoping that someone had cancelled their appointment, but this was not the case. She had to wait quite a while; this increased her anxiety level, she did not have the patience to wait very long. The chairs in the hall were all occupied, she was hoping they were not all waiting for Mr. Ricer. She was fortunate, her name was called, and this was good for Arial and everyone there. When she stood her legs were weak and wobbly, this was from fear. Mr. Ricer was seated at his desk, he smiled as she entered and asked her to be seated. Curiosity was killing Arial, she wanted him to get to the point.

He began by explaining that he had been in California for two weeks, he had attended a seminar that was related to homicide concerning mental patients. He continued to explain that he had acquired a tremendous amount of knowledge at the seminar. Due to the amount of information he had acquired from law enforcement and psychiatrist, the case would not be dismissed. The investigation would continue. Arial almost cried, she was so relieved, the thought of Don walking free was not an option. His life would be much shorter if he was released, that she was sure of.

# Chapter Twenty

## Tara's Autopsy Report

After a few months had passed, Arial had a deep need for a copy of Tara's autopsy report. People often thought that Arial was punishing herself for Tara's death. The autopsy report would reveal more than Arial needed to know, but she would not give up. She called the state medical records office in Crowleigh, the autopsy report was a matter of public record, anyone could request a copy.

The lady answered very casually, Arial explained what she wanted; there was information the lady needed to fill the request. She needed Tara's full name, birthdate, date of death, city and state where the death occurred. Then she needed Arial's information, address, and how they were related. Arial was then put on hold, and Arial despised to be put on hold. She hated to listen to elevator music, or recorded ads. Arial really just hated to wait, patience was not one of her greatest virtues. Then a voice returned to the phone, thank God, Arial thought. The lady informed Arial that the autopsy report was not fully complete, but as soon as the state coroner completed it, she would mail it to Arial immediately. There was only one thing that Arial could say, and that was thank you, and then she hung up. Arial was disappointed; she wanted it yesterday, not next month. Unfortunately for Arial it would be at least a month. She started checking the mailbox the next day. She watched for the mailman each day, it became an obsession for Arial, just like everything else in Arial's life that pertained to Tara. Every day she walked to the mail box, her head was usually pointed down, she never saw the outside world, it was almost as if there was not a world outside of her house. She remained secluded in her own little space, except for work; even there she was alone. Finally after repeated and repeated walks to the mail box, she opened the mail box and there it was, or at least she hoped it was. There was a return address from the State Medical's Office. She placed it against her chest and slowly walked to the house. Arial wanted to open it, but there was a fear of the unknown. She had never examined an autopsy report, and she was concerned about what it would contain. She lay it down for a while, she dreaded opening the envelope, she wanted to, but it would have to wait for her to gain enough strength to tear it open.

Arial tried to stay busy for a while, she made herself vacuum and dust, she definitely needed to do these household chores, she had gotten lazy, or at least that was what she thought. The reality was, Arial's depression was very serious, the drive and enthusiasm for life had disappeared. She was so tired, sleepy, anxious, her entire body was wound as tight as a rubber band. Each time she passed the envelope she paused and stared at it. She was alone in the house, it was quite, and maybe this would be the best time to open the envelope. Arial was feeling nauseated, she needed something cold to settle her stomach, she retrieved a diet drink from the refrigerator, lit a cigarette; that she did not need and sat down. She drank a few sips of the drink, she tried not to stare at the envelope, but the inevitable time had arrived. The suspense she was feeling was overwhelming. She had to open the envelope, it was securely packaged, and it required scissors to open. Arial's shaking hands did not help, but she finally managed to get inside. There were only a few pages; the first page consisted of Tara's name, age, address, place of death and cause of death. The cause of death was listed as a homicide. It also included the place the autopsy was performed and the medical examiner that performed it. The one item Arial desired was the time of death, it was addressed as unknown or the exact time could not be determined. Arial had her reasons for wanting the time of death.

The next page was an inferior drawing of a female body, front and back. There were lines drawn, each line showed a measurement; length, width, and depth. Each line represented each stab wound, and there were forty stab wounds. Tara's wounds began from the top of her head and continued downward to her lower torso, the wounds were located on the front and back side of her body. There were defense wounds located on her hands and arms, she did try to defend herself. Arial stared at the drawings and cried, realizing that she could not even begin to imagine the pain and fear that Tara endured.

The next page consisted of information that Arial could barely read. Arial was not aware of the process of an autopsy, there it was, written in a language that any one could comprehend. The organs were removed and weighed, the weight was included with each organ. The pancreas, intestines, liver and a few other organs had been removed. The bottom of the page included one more organ, the brain; this section was the part that Arial could not accept! They had removed her brain, the very core of her existence, the organ that controlled every aspect of Tara's life! This statement was more than Arial could cope with. Immediately the tears began to flow furiously from Arial's eyes, coating her cheeks with anguish, she could not read any longer, she placed the paperwork into the envelope and closed it securely. This information would have to wait until another day. Arial waited a couple of days to reexamine the autopsy report. Arial's memory was minimal at best; she had forgotten most of the information that was printed in the report. It was almost like starting over again. She sat at the kitchen table, which was where she spent most of her days when she was not working. She opened the envelope once more with the same amount of dread she felt previously. Arial had taken a nerve pill hoping it would help her get through this, she was feeling calmer, her attention span had seemed to improve slightly. She began on the first page, she read every word, she studied each word; she did not want to misunderstand a single word. This time she noticed Don's name typed as the spouse, what it did not say was that he was the alleged murderer. The second page, she paid close attention to each stab wound, each location, the measurement of each stab wound, and the superficial wounds which appeared to be defense wounds. The last page, as before upset Arial tremendously, the brain, was the same as the first time; it was as if this confirmed Tara's death. Somewhere deep within Arial, she hoped that all of the events that had occurred had been a terrible dream, and she would wake up and call Tara's phone number and she would answer. The night of Tara's death, the funeral, and all the other occurrences had not mentally sunk into her brain. The autopsy report was the final definite confirmation that her sister was gone from this earth.

The loss of a close family member can be devastating, but usually the people left behind on this earth deal with their grief and move on. Arial was not one of those fortunate people. Arial's loss was tremendous and the truth was that Arial did not want to move on. In Arial's mixed up mind, if she moved on it would be a betrayal to her sister.

# Chapter Twenty-One

## Arial's Visit with Don

One morning Arial was doing her usual things; nothing. Thinking, thinking and thinking, that was all she did, trying to make heads or tails of the entire situation. Tara was gone, Don was in jail and Arial was all screwed up. Why Dear God, did Don have to kill Tara? Tara was his only door to any form of recovery, he trusted her with every breathe he took. She loved him more than life itself, there was not anything that she would not do to help Don. Tara's complete life revolved around Don, then her children; as much as she loved her children, Don needed her more. He was always sick, and Tara was more aware of his need for her as each day passed.

The phone rang, it startled Arial; she was somewhere in her small world all alone. She answered the phone; it was Lela, Tara's daughter. Lela was working, but she had a question for Arial and she was not exactly sure how to ask. Lela began by asking Arial how she was coping? Arial lied and replied that she was improving. Lela was happy to hear that remark because she had a huge favor to ask Arial. Arial could not begin to imagine what huge favor Lela was about to ask. Lela was still having difficulty spitting the question from her mouth. Finally she gained enough courage to ask Arial if she would go with her to the jail to see Don? Lela heard silence, and then Arial explained that she did not know, she would have to consider it. Arial told Lela that she had another appointment with her psychiatrist the following week and she would discuss it with him. This satisfied Lela, Arial had not definitely said no, so maybe it was possible.

Arial sat there and wondered how or why Lela would even consider asking her to visit Don in jail? Lela knew exactly how Arial felt about Don. Lela and Arial had been to grief therapy together, both knew fully how the other one felt, and there were no hard feelings toward the other.

The following week Arial kept her appointment with her psychiatrist, she hated having to drive to Chanston but she did not have a choice. The trip was about fifty miles one-way, she rode in complete silence, but her brain was always working overtime. She could have turned the radio on, but the desire for music was gone. She just rode and watched cars fly past her, some people would nod their heads as they passed her, but Arial just ignored them. It seemed as if the common courtesy Arial once was endowed with had disappeared. She was not happy, therefore; she did not acknowledge other people as she once had. Arial did not care anymore about any aspect of life.

Arial finally arrived at the doctor's office, she did not want to get out of her car, she did not want to talk to this man, he disagreed with everything she said; and this pissed her off. She opened the car door and threw the cigarette she had been smoking and stomped on it. No smoking in the doctor's office! She entered, signed in, and sat down. Only a few moments passed and the patient before her exited, she knew she was next. Arial Greene, she heard her name called, oh; she dreaded this! The doctor was standing, he shook hands with her and asked her to be seated. The questions began; how was she, was she feeling any improvement and did she have any questions? Arial did not really reply to any of his questions except the last one; did she have any questions!

She began by explaining Lela's peculiar request; at least she thought it was peculiar. The doctor actually agreed with her for once, he also thought it was peculiar. Once again, he suggested that the final decision was Arial's. He was not thrilled with the idea, he was concerned with what Arial's reaction would be when she laid her eyes on Don. There was a suspicion that the guards might have to forcibly escort Arial out! He continued to say that if she thought it might help her in any way; she should go. He wanted her to implement a lot of thought before she made a final decision. That was his answer to everything.

Psychiatrist, what good are they? They sit there and listen, ask questions, and oh yeah; they can write a prescription. Arial was told that she did not want to get better, she had made a shrine, he wanted her to remove every picture of Tara, or anything in her house that would remotely cause Arial to think about Tara! The psychiatrist could not possibly place himself in Arial's mind. Arial did not need material items to remember Tara, she only had to open her eyes each morning and that was the first thing that entered her mind before her feet hit the floor! Something funny or sad, stupid or smart, it did not matter at all, she just had to open her eyes!

Arial thought to herself, he has never been this close to anyone in his entire life. She thought that he probably needed to see a psychiatrist because he had never allowed himself to have such a unique relationship with any one. He had probably lived a lonely life, if it could be compared with the uniqueness of Tara's and Arial's life. Then from nowhere; it was taken away, there was absolutely not any way he would ever understand!

It really did not matter to Arial what his thoughts were, she fully intended to do as she pleased as it pertained to Tara. There was one thing for sure, she was going to place a lot of thought into the idea of visiting Don, she really did not want to get arrested for losing her cool at the jail.

Arial had to do a lot of soul searching, crying and she talked to Tara about the dilemma she was in. When she talked to Tara, she tried to explain that the only reason she was even considering the thought of visiting Don was to see his reaction and to feel hers. She knew that Tara and Don had loved each other, but something went terribly wrong the night Tara died. The guilt Arial felt concerning Tara's death had completely overwhelmed Arial. She honestly felt like it should have been her that had died, Tara was such a good person, and the world loved her so much. Tara deserved to live a life free from Don and his sickness, free to laugh, free to know that when she arrived home there would be peace and a quietness she so deserved. Tara was gone now and she would never have that joy. This realization caused Arial severe anxiety and nausea just to know that Tara had lived a life consumed with dread and doubt. Most of their marriage was pleasant enough except for Don's depression.

Arial thought and remembered how much Tara actually loved Don, even with the constant ups and downs of Don's true mental illness, she chose to remain married to him never once imagining the degree of instability Don's mental illness would escalate to, or the untimely immature end of her life. Arial finally had to make a decision, one that she was not certain about; she decided to call Lela and agree to her request to visit Don.

Lela was surprised, but happy Arial had agreed to visit her dad. Lela made the arrangements, and a few days later they met at the county jail. Arial made a promise to herself that she would retain her composure. Arial arrived before Lela, she remained in her car, she sat there and watched as family members entered and exited the jail, and there were a large number of visitors. Most of the people entering for a visit appeared to be very poor, Arial thought this mainly because of their appearance. They appeared dirty, clothes unkempt, and then Arial thought, do not judge these people by their appearance, she thought; I do not have a lot of money, I could be considered poor, so she shifted her thoughts. The jail was a brick building with probably twelve feet fencing surrounding the building. There were armed guards around the building, she was thinking that Don was safer inside the jail than he would be if he was free and outside those walls.

Lela was late, but Arial knew she would be there, but she better speed it up before Arial changed her mind. Arial did not like sitting there, this was a bad part of town, she checked her doors to reassure herself that they were locked. She turned sideways in her seat, as she did she saw Lela drive in. Arial waved at her, she thought, she is such a good niece. Lela had loved her mother so much; this was so very difficult for her. Lela's dad had killed her mother, but she was honestly trying to understand, to forgive, She absolutely could not separate her parents. Arial was trying to understand, if not; she would not be waiting to visit Don. Lela was smiling; she was beautiful; long blonde hair, slim, but Arial could see her red eyes, she had been crying. Lela was as frightened as Arial was, Lela had no idea what type of reaction Arial would display when she saw Don, and this concerned Lela. Arial opened her car door to greet Lela, they hugged and took a deep breathe.

They entered the door and asked for Don by name, there was a glass partition with chairs on their side. They stood, both were too nervous to sit, a door opened from the other side of the glass, it was Don; he was crying. He had been positive that he would never see Arial again except in a courtroom, but there she was. Arial stared at him, she did not know what she expected, but there was Don, her brother-in-law; the same man she had always liked, she had always felt sorry for him because of his mental illness, and then tears began to flow from Arial's eyes. She actually felt sorry for him, she could not hear him but she could read his lips, he repeated the same words over and over; "I AM SO SORRY", and Arial believed him. Don then placed the palm of his hand on the glass, by this time Arial was truly crying, she placed her hand on the glass over Don's hand and she completely fell apart. The guilt Arial felt was more than she could could cope with; she told Lela she would wait for her outside. Arial felt like she had betrayed Tara's memory beyond repair. Arial was feeling sorry for herself, she wanted her sister back, she wanted all of this to disappear, and she wanted her life to return to normal, and that meant that Tara would answer the phone when she called her.

A few minutes passed and Lela came outside, of course she had been crying profusely. She thanked Arial for coming, she was positive that her dad felt much better. Arial hugged Lela, said good-by, but they both knew that Arial would never return, and Lela understood, she was just thankful for this one time.

The visitation with Don had not helped Arial, it only increased her anxiety level to the point that she had to take an extra anti-anxiety pill. Arial sat down and did not move for several hours. She dozed off from the extra pill, but she needed that rest, she was so strung out and tired from her visit with Don, the extra sleep helped her, even if she was sleeping sitting straight up. She was alone in the house and it was quite, there were no interruptions.

# Chapter Twenty-Two

## Time Passes On

Arial's attitude improved with time as she continued taking her wonder pill, her anti-depressant, this became very noticeable especially at work. Once again she could operate her job proficiently, and she was talking to everyone. She did not smile as often as she once did, but she was improving. Tara was the only thing that she thought about, sometimes this aided with her job performance. Arial would be so mad, she worked harder, this seemed to be a release for Arial; almost a method of releasing her anger. She would be so tired at the end of her shift, but the depression increased the tiredness. Arial dreaded going home; she would be totally alone there, which is really what she desired. The house could be filled with people, her husband, her kids, grandchildren, it did not make any difference; she was still alone. Arial had always heard these words; a person can be in a room filled with people, but still be alone, now she understood the meaning of those words.

Arial's few friends and family members continued to check on her regularly, they were all aware that Arial was not well. She was not left alone for very long, they knew her mind was still screwed up, and they wondered about suicide; they had always been concerned about this possibility.

Arial's marriage was on the rocks, she had no desire to even see his car when it pulled into the driveway. She would avoid him at any cost. Tara's death had changed Arial's attitude, the rage that had been locked inside her, well that door had been opened and she did not care anymore. Arial had not loved Clark in many years, she had been playing a game of charades for the sake of her children for many years and Clark did not have a clue. She had made a mistake twenty years ago, just one mistake; and it would follow her to her grave. She had hurt her children so terribly and Clark also. She was so sorry for what she had done because of her children, not for Clark. The love was gone and she tried but she could never manage to mend her marriage. Tara would laugh at Arial and then scold her. Two sisters, two grown women, completely the opposite in character. Tara tried to explain her thoughts as to why Arial had an affair. Tara would say, Arial, you never had a life, your entire life has been isolated and controlled by someone else. You just sat back and allowed the world to tromp all over you. This man triggered something in you that you did not know existed; life! He made you feel wanted and needed, and then she said, I am not going to tell you that he loved you, because he probably did not, but I am sure he had a great time with you for the last two years. Those last few words hurt Arial so badly; she had fallen in love with this man, a true love, a love that never diminishes.

Tara said the affair was probably very good for Arial; it had given her joy, excitement, something to look forward to daily, even if it was just a phone call. Tara had always given her honest opinion, if you liked it great, if not, that was also great, she really did not care. If Arial asked a question of Tara, she received the truth. Tara ended that particular conversation by informing Arial that she had enjoyed enough adrenaline rushes for that time in her life. Arial was not happy about the situation, but her kids were her first priority in life. Arial meant that she would go to any extreme, to make sure her children lived and were raised in what everyone thought was a good home. Arial completed this act of love, it took twenty-five years to accomplish this. Arial did not want an award of any sorts, she only wanted her children to be happy. She did not do anything special, she only did what any loving mother would do.

# Chapter Twenty-Three

## The District Attorney Call

Arial had not heard from the District Attorney in about a week, some process of the judicial system had to be occurring; she just did not know what. She had tried not to call the D,A. but as usual her lack of patience was getting the best of her. So of course she made that phone call, and of course; he was in court, she had to leave a message. Later in the day, the D.A. did return her call, not out of any courtesy, but he needed to talk to all of them. He refrained from explaining the reason over the phone, it had to be in person. Once again Arial's anxiety level began to rise; she wanted to know yesterday, not tomorrow! It was a futile attempt, he refused; in person, all of them at the same time and that was final! Arial called her brother's to explain, they were as anxious as she was. The appointment was the next day; all of them had to make special arrangements concerning their work, but it all worked out. They all arrived on time, but separately. They walked slowly, discussing every possibility, neither of them having a clue, maybe Don was sick, or dead, that was their preference.

They entered Mr. Ricer's office, he offered them a seat, and then he paused; he knew this conversation was going to be difficult, his only recourse was to spit it out. He was concerned about Arial's reaction, she was going to explode. He gazed at her and she was staring at him with a what the crap facial expression. He began slowly, he explained that Don had agreed to a guilty plea of second degree murder, Arial's mouth fell open. What did he mean second degree? Don had killed Tara, her sister; and he was going to get away with second degree murder! Arial's voice began to reach a higher volume! Mr. Ricer knew this would happen; he had talked to Arial enough over the last two years to predict her reaction. Tara's brother's just sat there with a bewildered expression on their face. Arial demanded answers, would there not be a trial? Why were they not informed concerning this so called deal?

Mr. Ricer began his thorough explanation, if there was a jury trial, there was always a chance of an acquittal because of Don's mental status. If the defense attorney entered a plea of guilty by means of insanity, this could really cause a problem. If Don was found guilty of murder, by means of insanity, this could possibly mean he would be sent to a mental hospital. If in time he was declared sane within any length of time, at least ninety days; he could be released back into society, and then he would be a free man. He explained that the jury could be very unpredictable, with Don's medical history, and it was a lifelong history, the jury would definitely take this into consideration. This equation definitely was cause for concern. Arial and her brother's sat with an expression of astonishment on their faces. Arial's thoughts were if Don was ever released he would be dead within a week, her brother's would make sure of that! This could not be allowed to happen. If this happened her brother's would be in jail for murder, probably for the rest of their lives. Arial immediately asked how long Don would serve for second degree murder, Mr. Ricer replied, "nine to fifteen years, with a reduction of time already served." This meant he could possibly be released in seven to thirteen years. This was not good, but Mr. Ricer explained that seven to thirteen years was better than a possible ninety days or a not guilty verdict. Don would pay some time for the murder of Tara.

Arial and her brother's stared at each other, was there not any other solution than this? Apparently not, they assumed that Mr. Ricer was trying to get some justice for Don's horrendous act. Arial continued to think about her brothers, what if Don did eventually get released, she knew her brother's to well, she was fully aware of what they were capable of, and she knew they would discover a way to end Don's life. This was her concern for the moment.

The deal had already been offered to Don and he had accepted, Mr. Ricer said that Don was so consumed with guilt he would have taken a first degree murder deal, but they honestly did not believe that it was premeditated. Truthfully, Arial agreed with that. She wanted him to pay for killing her sister; he could not be allowed to walk away without any punishment at all. Mr. Ricer was waiting patiently for some kind of verbal response, Arial and her brother's had been sitting and thinking to themselves. Their preconceived thoughts were that the family had to be notified and agree with a deal before it was offered to the defendant; in this case, Don. The deal had been offered to Don first, he accepted, and then the family was contacted, something seemed to be wrong with the picture. Arial thought that maybe the laws had been changed, or the moral issues had been disregarded; either way the deal seemed to have been set in stone, and for good reasons. They all finally agreed with the end result.

Arial asked when this hearing would be, he simply replied that he would call her as soon as he was informed. Arial and her brother's stood to leave, they thanked Mr. Ricer, and he assured Arial he would call her. They left the office in a foul mood, as they walked the halls of the court house; it seemed so large, large concrete and what appeared to be marble or granite walls and floors, a substantially grand décor they were sure cost millions to create, as far as they were concerned they could have hung Don on the court square and saved a lot of money. Time had changed things, there was more concern for the defendant than for the victim. The victim seemed to have no rights at all. Tara, Arial's only sister had been murdered and Don would receive very little punishment for her death.

# Chapter Twenty-Four

## The Final Hearing

Arial's wait for Mr. Ricer's call would be longer than she had anticipated. Arial's patience was very thin, so thin she really wanted to go in the back yard and scream as loudly as she possibly could. She did reconsider that idea, the neighbors thought she was crazy, that would certainly reconfirm their thoughts. The justice system was so slow, Arial realized that the system was severely back logged by a minimum of two years, probably more, but gracious; how long would a plea hearing actually last. Arial was worried about the unknown, what if, what if this, what if everything, she wanted it to be over and done with. She wanted Don behind bars in a permanent facility, away from the vicinity of any general public. It happened once, if he was ever released, it could happen again.

Finally, after what seemed to be a month, Mr. Ricer called, the hearing date had been set. It was so long ago, Arial had forgotten the exact date, but it was only a couple of weeks away. That couple of weeks felt like a life time. The date finally arrived, Arial, her brother's, and her mother descended upon the courthouse. They were so anxious, especially Arial, even at this hearing she wanted to be seated where she could see Don and he could see her. She wanted him to know that she had not forgiven him, and she never would. Don knew this and he was really sorry, but Arial did not care, he had killed her sister, he had taken away one of the most important things in her life; and he had to pay.

The judge came in once again; there he sat with that big hammer, high above everyone else, Arial did respect the judge but he seemed to give off an essence that implied that he was better than anyone else in the courtroom. The judge spoke to the defense attorney, and then the prosecution, then he asked Don to stand. The judge asked Don if he understood what was occurring within the courtroom, Don replied softly that he did understand. The judge asked Don if he was aware that he was entitled to a jury trial, Don replied yes. Don was also asked if he had been coerced in anyway or by anyone to accept a second degree murder charge, he replied no.

The judge began to explain the consequences of the plea deal. Don would serve a sentence of nine to fifteen years, with a reduction of two years for time served. Don would be placed in a prison that provided mental care. The exact location had not been determined. The judge instructed Don that he would be returned to the county jail until a prison had been selected. Then the judge pounded that huge hammer and announced that court was over!

Don's parents were older and their health was not good, they did ask that Don be placed in a prison that was close enough for them to visit, the judge agreed to their request. Later Don was sent to a prison that was located about forty miles from Kingston, this was still quite a distance for Don's parents, but that was the closest prison that included a mental ward. It was probably a month before Don was transferred to the prison. Arial was delighted when that day arrived.

Arial thought that the end of this entire event would allow closure to begin, but that was not the case, for Arial there would never be complete closure.

# Chapter Twenty-Five

## The Retrieval of Tara's Clothes

Arial's life continued on, she had improved some, enough to live a somewhat normal life. She was still consumed with rage, and hate. The previous Arial was gone, the new Arial did not care about anything or anybody. She wanted her sister back, she was so alone, Arial's sweet personality had been transformed into a bitch, and she did not care.

A few months had passed and Arial wondered if the police department had retained Tara's clothes, she wanted them back; there was one shirt that Arial had purchased at the beach for Tara, on the front was a picture of a little girl, and it read; I am the little sister. This shirt had never been accounted for, Arial was sure that Tara was wearing it the night she died. She called the police department, explained who she was and what she wanted. Arial was immediately connected to another department, this transfer was the appropriate department. This was the records department, Arial once again had to repeat what she wanted, he had to check to make sure it was available, it only took him a few minutes to locate the articles. He returned to the phone and informed Arial that she could pick them up at any time. She assured him she would be there shortly.

Arial was anxious, but she wanted that shirt and she was positive it was there. She was in a flutter, in a hurry as always. Quickly she got in her car, driving faster than normal, when she arrived at the courthouse, the parking lot was full; this aggravated Arial. She rode around and around, hoping someone would leave. Finally after about five drive a rounds she spotted a car backing out, and she was determined to get it. The cars lined up behind would just have to wait. Finally she pulled in, now what? Arial sat there dreading to enter the court house, she wanted the clothes, but she did not know what to expect. She noticed that cars were slowing down, assuming she was going to back out, so she decided to get out of her car; it was now or never. Arial had no idea where to go, she stopped at the first window she saw, thankfully they knew exactly where to send her. Arial had to wait for a policeman to arrive, but it only took a minute. he asked Arial's name, and the name of the defendant, Arial also asked to see the photos taken at the scene. The policeman paused for a moment, and then replied that he needed to make a phone call. He was only gone for a moment, but when he returned he told her that he had called Mr. Ricer, the D.A. Mr. Ricer instructed the policeman to tell Arial to call him before she looked at the pictures. The policeman stared at Arial, he felt sorry for her, she looked so sad; he tried to explain that if she viewed the pictures taken at the scene, that would be how she would remember Tara for the rest of her life. He went on to say that he was not trying to hide anything from her, he wanted her to remember her sister the way she looked the last time Arial saw her alive. Arial just stood there silently, she was wondering why, but she realized that she should not view the pictures. Arial asked for Tara's clothes, the policeman did not question her any more, he opened the door to the evidence room and proceeded to locate Tara's clothes. Arial did get a brief view inside the room, it was cluttered; she wondered how he could possibly find anything in there. He returned quickly, in his hand he carried a small brown bag, the top of the bag was rolled downward about halfway. He placed it on a table, Arial immediately reached for it, she opened it and placed her hand inside, she felt cloth; she closed the bag as quickly as she opened it. She thanked the policeman and left the building. Arial's hands were shaking, she wanted the clothes, but she was afraid to look at them. As she walked to her car, she lit a cigarette; she knew this was a no smoking area, the entire lot; but at that moment she did not care. The parking lot was still full, cars were circling the lot hoping to find a close parking space, there were none. It was such a pretty day, a little brisk, but a day anyone would enjoy being outside, except Arial. She sat in her car for a few moments, staring at the brown bag she had placed in the seat beside her. She was determined not to open it until she returned home. Arial continued to view the world outside her car, maybe somewhere deep within Arial she really wanted to enjoy life once more, but the guilt she carried inside her heart would not allow it. The sadness and depression had taken over Arial, even with her wonder pill; her anti-depressant, she was not well, better; but far from well! Arial thought well she had to go home sometime, it may as well be now. She finally backed out of her parking spot, a car behind her was very anxious, Arial could see his face from her rear view mirror, he was ticked off. She did not care about that either, in fact; she did not care about anything.

When Arial arrived home, the house was empty and quiet, that was a blessing, she wanted to be alone when she opened that brown bag. She placed the bag on the table, she really needed to use the bathroom first, she did not want to be interrupted by anything as she was inspecting the contents.

She returned from the bathroom and sat down at the table, she knew the contents of the bag would not hurt her physically, but she was wondering how much more her brain could accept. Arial knew she was going to open the bag and soon, while she was alone. She gently reached for the bag and began to unroll it, she did not want to disturb anything inside. She easily reached inside the bag, she felt the cloth; carefully she removed it; there it was, the shirt. It was turned inside out just as the coroner had removed it from Tara's small body. Even from the inside there was dried blood, slashes in the shirt. Arial thought, oh Lord, there is a hair, she quickly snatched the hair, she did not want to lose it, that was a small piece of Tara she had in her possession. Arial began to carefully turn the shirt, it also was rolled like the bag, she finally finished turning the shirt, and sure enough there was the cartoon character displaying the words I am the little sister! Arial began to cry, it was covered with blood, and so many slashes from the knife Don had used to kill her. Arial discovered several more curly hairs on the shirt, she had to be very careful handling the shirt, she refused to lose even one hair. This shirt was all she had left of her sister, she cuddled the shirt, placed it to her face; she could smell her scent, and this made the tears flow. Arial had purchased the shirt for Tara at the beach, she remembered her wearing it to work, the memories began to come back, silly things and remarks that Tara had said; and the hilarious adventures they had shared. These special memories did bring a smile to Arial's face. She very carefully rerolled the shirt, she was very careful to watch for every hair, making sure that not one was lost.

Arial noticed that the bag was standing upright; she wondered if there was anything else in the bag. She carefully placed the shirt on the table, and then she reached inside the bag again. She felt something, it was smaller than the shirt, it also was rolled; she had no idea what it was, she was beginning to feel the anxiety build, she had just calmed down a little, now here was something else. Whatever it was she knew she had to be very careful. Slowly she placed her hand around the object firmly and removed it from the bag. Oh my God, it was her panties. The panties were also exactly as the coroner had removed them. They were also rolled inside out, Arial could see the blood stains before she unrolled them. They were so small, almost like a child's. Arial began to unroll the panties, the tears began once more. Arial had always heard that when a person dies that sometimes the organs relax and the bladder may empty after death. This had happened, there were urine stains all over Tara's panties, Arial assumed that this had happened after Tara had passed, but she wondered; Tara was going to the bathroom when Don stabbed her the first time, she could have urinated before she died. Arial's mind was all screwed up, sometimes thoughts would wonder around in Arial's head that did not matter or were not even related to the actual death of her sister. She wanted answers and she had never received a definite reason for her death.

She examined every inch of those small panties, there were pubic hairs attached, she did not want to lose those either. After a full examination of the panties she rerolled them and placed the shirt and panties inside the bag and closed it securely. She had to find a location in the house that would assure their safety. She stared around the kitchen and living room, nothing or anywhere popped out to her. She began to walk the house, room to room, there had to be somewhere safe! Suddenly she remembered the closet where she kept all the paperwork concerning Tara. The furnace was in that closet but there was a shelf that she had loaded down with paperwork, no one ever bothered that area; Arial thought they were frightened to touch any of her papers, they never knew what kind of reaction she would reveal, and they did not know how to deal with her, so they just left her alone. No one would even talk to Arial about Tara's death; and this was a mistake, she was so alone, and this meant that she had to keep all of her thoughts and fears deep within herself.

The closet was the ideal location for Tara's clothes; she placed them on the far back of the shelf, but she checked frequently to reassure herself they were safe. Of course opening that door caused an overwhelming urge to reread all the paperwork, There she sat for several hours rehashing every gruesome detail of Tara's death and the aftermath that had followed. She seemed to have no control, she was always afraid that she had missed something important, one little item that would say that Don had planned to kill Tara. She was constantly digging for that one piece of evidence that would swallow Don completely. It should not have even mattered to Arial at that time, Don had accepted a plea, he was in prison, he could not be tried for Tara's death, it was over. It was over for Don and the judicial system, it had ended; but it would never end for Arial.

# Chapter Twenty-Six

## Arial's Obession

Arial's life did continue, she went to work, did housework, played with her grandchildren, she did all the things any other woman did on any given day. There were problems with depression, it never completely went away. Arial decided that she wanted to dedicate one room in her house to Tara. Clark, her husband; he was at a loss. He did not want to deal with Arial's wild ideas; he just stood back and let her do whatever she wanted. She did not ask for permission, those days were gone; the control Clark once held over Arial was gone. She did and went as she pleased, and Clark quickly discovered not to even ask or suggest an explanation for anything she did.

There was one room in the house that was not used, their middle son had married and moved out. Arial became obsessed with the makeover of this room. Tara loved the color yellow, and she had loved yellow rose buds. Arial found the perfect shade of yellow for the walls, and then she searched for a wall paper border that would match the walls; and she found it. Arial's son that had married had only left one thing in the room, it was a fish aquarium; a large one with only one fish. It was a beautiful fish, but Arial wanted the aquarium removed. Arial began her painting, and each time her son came by the house, Arial would remind him that she was painting the room and that she was painting around the aquarium; but when she reached that area the fish and aquarium better be gone or she would remove it herself. Her son did not take her seriously, he never thought for one moment that his mom would hurt his fish. Arial continued to paint and one day there she was; the only area not painted was around the aquarium. She stood back and gazed at the beautiful fish, she really hated to do it, but she had warned him what seemed to be a million times what would happen. Poor little fish, it was not his fault; but neither was it Arial's. The aquarium held a large amount of water, she had to put some thought into this; how would she ever remove all that water? Arial began her search, she thought about siphoning the water using a water hose, but she knew she would have to use her mouth to start a flow of water, that idea went straight out the window; yuck, she could not do that. She went outside and looked around, there was a dirty bucket in the utility building, that might work. Arial knew she would have to dip the water by hand; she was worried about the mess; there was carpet in that room. She hunted until she found a pitcher, and then she began to dip. The poor little fish, he was scared to death, Arial felt sorry for him; he did not realize that he was going to die. She had been warning her son for probably a month, he did not listen; so Arial was going to empty that tank. Bucket after bucket, it took a while but finally Arial removed all the water from the tank. The last bucket of water she saved to put the fish in, she knew the poor little thing would not make it and she was sorry. Arial carried the bucket with the fish in it outside, she had no idea what else to do with it.

There was the empty, nasty fish tank, it was glass and it was heavy, but Arial was determined to remove it. The tank was sitting on a wooden stand, the stand would be easy, but that tank would prove to be a problem. She began by pushing and pulling the tank forward until there was only a small portion remaining on the stand, she was holding it up. Arial moved backwards, still holding the tank; slowly she let it slide until her end was tilted on the floor. She continued to hold it as she moved to the other end, she did not want it to break, it would probably cut her foot off. She lifted the other end and struggled to place it on the floor, that darn thing was heavy. She had placed a towel on the floor before she began that nasty quest. She grabbed the towel and pulled it slowly to the back door, that was going to be another struggle; the cement in the garage. Arial actually accomplished her task without breaking the glass tank, she was so proud of herself. But then there was the fish, she knew it did not have much oxygen left and it would die. Morally, Arial did struggle with that, but not for long, she still had a lot of work to do. The tank stand was easy; she just pushed it out the back door. She cleaned up the mess and looked around. Arial spoke out loud to Tara, her sister; it will not take me to much longer to complete your room, she knew that Tara would like the room. This room was just for the two of them and it was almost completed.

Clark, Arial's husband, such as he was; came home that day before he went to play golf, when he realized that the fish tank was gone, he was upset, but he did not say anything. Arial looked at him, she could almost see the little horns protruding from his head, but he kept quite; he did not want Arial to go into a rage. He got his golf clubs and left. Arial did not care what he thought or where he went, she was glad he had left, she wanted to be alone, all by herself, she seemed to have a need to wallow in her own self pity.

Later in the day Arial's son and his wife came by for a visit, when they entered Arial was sitting on the sofa relaxing, she was tired; she had been working all day. They came in laughing and handed Arial her granddaughter. This little girl had added an extreme amount of pleasure to Arial's life. Arial softened when she held this bundle of joy. Arial's son was going toward his old bedroom, when he reached the hall and turned toward his room he could see the fish tank was gone. Whoa, he could not believe that Arial had emptied the tank! He was so shocked; his wife stared at him; she could not believe her ears! Arial had been warning him for at least a month what would happen. He just could not believe that his mom would do that, but she did. He did get over it.

Arial continued decorating the room, she put up the rose border, and finished painting. She was so proud; she knew Tara would love it. She needed furniture, off to town she went. Arial was excited; she wanted this room to be perfect, what she thought Tara would enjoy spending time in. She went from one furniture store to another, her excitement was beginning to diminish, she could not find what she wanted. This was the last store, and then she had to go home. She knew exactly what she wanted, but she had not found it yet. She was browsing throughout the store when a salesman asked if he could assist her. Arial began to describe what she was looking for, the salesman smiled and asked her to follow him. She followed him to the back of the store to a back room, which really appeared to be a junk room. There it was, in the very back of the room, a sofa with yellow roses everywhere, and a chair to match, this really got Arial's adrenaline hopped up! She turned to the salesman and smiled, she instructed him to move everything, she wanted the sofa and chair. This thrilled the salesman, they had never expected to ever sale these two items. The furniture was new, but it was so loud, the background color was a dark teal green, and those yellow roses, well let's just say it was a little too much for most people's taste. He could see the glow in Arial's face, as if she had won a grand prize! Regardless of what he thought, this lady was deliriously happy, so he gave her a discount, not a lot but enough to make her smile more joyful. When she left the store the salesman said that she was probably the most satisfied customer he ever had. He had no idea why that furniture made her so happy, if he had known he probably would have given her a larger discount.

The furniture was delivered, Arial would stand and stare into the room, to Arial it was the grandest room she had ever seen. She had a television, she could watch what she wanted without being bothered by anyone, this was her room to share with Tara, she did not want anyone else in there. There were pictures of Tara in several places; some were of Tara and Arial, she was so proud to say that Tara was her sister, and she was so depressed knowing that she was no longer with her.

The room that Arial had made into a shrine for Tara was probably the worst thing for her sanity that she could have done. Arial's mental status was not quite up to par, even with the anti-depressant. It was a constant reminder, but Arial honestly thought that it gave her comfort and peace. She would sit and cry as she would relive every precious moment she shared with Tara. Arial thought the crying was good for her, she assumed it was a release of some of her anguish and guilt, She was so wrong, that room only counteracted any pleasantness she had in her life.

The death of a dearly beloved person is devastating for anyone. Each person deals with death in different ways, most people can function normally in their everyday life. They miss the person that was taken, but they realize they have to move on. But sometimes there are people like Arial who for whatever reason cannot cope as well as others. Arial had so much guilt because she was left here on this earth and Tara was taken away far too soon.

The psychiatrist Arial continued to see would get so aggravated with her, he tried at each visit to explain to Arial that she did not want to get better. Of course Arial denied that observation, she was there talking to him, she explained that she did want to get better, otherwise she would not be there. The only person that Arial was fooling was herself, she knew that she was lying to the psychiatrist, but she did not want him to know. He knew, and he was at a loss as how to help her. Arial refused to redo the room, she refused to remove Tara's pictures, and they usually ended up arguing at each visit. He decided that Arial needed grief therapy just with a psychologist. Arial jumped at that, the doctor and Arial had never quite connected; Arial would not budge and the doctor absolutely could not budge her. He recommended a grief therapist, a lady, Arial felt that a woman would understand her grief more thoroughly than a man. She expected a lady therapist to be more compassionate, and understanding; so she agreed with his suggestion. He scheduled the appointment for the following week, at the same time Arial was thinking, this is good, I will not have to see your face again and listen to your accusations. Appointment in hand, Arial said her final good-bye to this man she did not like. The truth was and Arial knew this, the reason she did not like him was because he was truly trying to help her, but she did not want his help. She was afraid to get better, this to Arial was a betrayal to Tara. Arial continued to suffer quietly in her own space, most of the time she was alone. She basically made this clear to her family, especially Clark, and he was more than thrilled with that prospect. He could not and did not want to deal with Arial concerning Tara's death.

# Chapter Twenty-Seven

## Clark and Arial's Life After Tara' Death

Arial had changed so much since Tara's death; her personality was almost the exact opposite. She was so full of rage, it was almost as if she hated the world, and she did did not care to express her feelings, which was most definitely the opposite. Arial had always been quiet and did as she was told, especially where Clark; her husband was concerned. He had managed to have control over Arial their entire marriage. Arial allowed this to occur, and for some reason she could not stop it. There was always a fear, a feeling of uncertainty, walking on egg shells, afraid to speak, never knowing what type of reaction Clark would produce.

Arial's love for Clark had been gone for many years, but she stayed, at first for her children, later in life; because she seemed to be in a rut. Just stuck, nowhere to go; so she remained with a man that she did not even like, much less love.

This type of life is totally useless for anyone, no affection, not caring if he ever came home, actually hoping that he would never return. Arial had always jumped each and every time Clark spoke.

Arial's love for Clark died early in the marriage, but there were four children, she did what she thought was best for their children. It was the best plan for her children and she has never regretted one moment of the choices she made. It was not fair to Arial, neither was it fair to Clark, she lived a lie, but she gave her marriage every chance there was to rebuild itself; but it never happened. The love was completely gone and it was very difficult living with a man that she did not love.

Tara's death had brought forth such hatred, meanness, sarcasm, and more loneliness than she had felt before Tara's death. Arial was truly alone, Tara was gone, her children were grown and married, and Clark; well he had better things to do than sit around with a depressed wife. He simply left Arial alone; he did not want to deal with her and he most certainly did not know how. Clark did not understand depression, most people; like Clark think a person can just snap out of it, well unfortunately that is not how it works. Arial suffered alone, but she did not care, she wanted to be alone, she wanted to die.

Arial went about her usual daily routine, day after day. She was so unhappy and alone. Frequently, Arial thoughts wandered to the one man in her past and present that she had ever truly loved, the man she had an affair with twenty or more years ago. She had not seen or talked to this man for more than twenty-five years, but that love Arial felt for him many years ago was still within her. Over the years, there would be times she would think about him, she would be so sad; she could not see him, it was as if a nauseated sick feeling would consume her. Before Tara's death, she knew how Arial felt about this man. Tara had been Arial's only confidant in life, the one person Arial knew she could trust with her innermost feelings. Tara was aware that Arial had not loved Clark for many years, she also knew that Arial was in love with another man. a man that she could not see ever again. Tara kept this secret and took it with her to her grave.

It was about four years after Tara's death, Arial had changed grocery stores, she began going to one of the big super centers, the prices were much lower, but she hated that store; she only went for groceries but that store had everything. She would get so aggravated, other customers would completely stop in an aisle, that meant Arial had to stop. Arial was always in a hurry, she had no patience at all, she often wanted to run over those people with her grocery cart, but she did not. One day she went grocery shopping, as usual she was in a hurry, she had to get home! If she was gone to long Clark would accuse her of being with another man. She was walking down the bread aisle, it was crowded and she was not paying any attention except to reach for what she needed. As she walked, someone caught her eye, before she realized who it was she had taken probably ten steps, suddenly; without any knowledge or reason she turned around and gazed behind herself. That exact moment she did not know why she turned around, but when she turned, a man had turned around, he was staring at her; it took a moment to recognize him. Twenty something years had made a lot of difference, but it was the same face, just aged a little, and a little weight gain; it was him, the man she had loved for so long! Each backed up to speak, she could not believe it. He almost did not recognize her, Arial had added a few pounds also. They were amazed, neither could believe it, he thought she had dropped off the face of the earth, or at least that is what he said. Arial felt her heart pounding, he looked so good, she felt as if she looked like a pile of crap. She had gained weight, not fat; but heavier. She was very self-conscious concerning the way she looked. Arial was frightened, she was so afraid that someone would see her talking to him and then call Clark. She was terrified, she wanted to talk longer but she absolutely could not! She told him that life had been good to him, he replied the same to her, and it was true, he looked just great!

Arial moved quickly, she was elated, she had not seen him for so many years, but she knew that had to get away from him quickly. Clark knew everyone in town, all it would take would be just one phone call, someone saying they had seen her talking to a man at the store. She could not handle the stress. She hurriedly completed her grocery shopping, but she glanced at each turn, hoping to see him one more time. She finished and tried to find an empty register, she was still glancing, hoping to spot him, and she did; but he did not see her.

She drove home; she knew that as soon as she got home she would call him. Arial remembered his phone number, she called his phone and as she did her hands began to shake; what was she doing? She did not allow enough time for reasoning to occur, she just called him, but he had not arrived home yet. Arial started to put the groceries up. She managed to finish the grocery chore, and then she sat and waited.

Clark was at work; her brain began to work overtime, what if Clark discovered this innocent incident? Arial began to wonder about her marriage, she did not love Clark, that was a fact, but their marriage had not been all bad. They had produced four beautiful children. There had been some good times; Clark could be a good husband if he chose to; but this was very seldom. Their children were grown with children of their own, it was just Clark and Arial now, the nest was empty. She dreaded to see him drive into the garage. She had so much resentment built up inside her towards Clark, if only she had enough guts to stand up to him, their marriage probably would not have lasted as long as it did. Clark meant that he would have full control over Arial, she never understood this, why? When they married Arial was so young, she was so stupid, she had seen the signs before they were married, but from lack of sense, the need to get away from her parents, whatever the reasons were, she married Clark, she had just turned seventeen. Immediately, that night the turmoil began, and it never completely ended, there would be a few good days, but that fear Arial could not let go of was always there.

When Tara died; Arial changed, she was so tired, and mad 24/7 she informed Clark that she would not jump at any of his commands any longer. She informed him that those days were gone, he was not an invalid, he would begin doing for himself, or do without; this time Arial meant every word she said. She was sure that Clark thought that she would not follow through with those worthless threats, but this time Clark was very badly mistaken, Arial ignored him, he would actually ask her to get him a glass of water. She told him he knew where the kitchen was at, if he wanted it; he would get it himself! Clark thought that Arial was testing him and that she would eventually give in; never happened.

Arial thought backwards into their marriage, he had never did anything for her, even if she was truly sick, to the point of a high fever, vomiting, dysentery, chest cold, it did not matter; he would tell her to go out in the cold and get her own medicine, because he was not going. Arial had thought numerous times that Clark would not have cared if she had died.

The bad outnumbered the good, People on the outside had no idea what was actually happening behind closed doors, and Arial was so ashamed of herself for not having the guts to tell anyone except Tara. Tara was aware of everything that was happening behind those doors. She felt sorry for Arial, but Arial had made the decision to remain in the marriage.

Arial had a secret savings account; Clark had no knowledge of its existence. Arial directed the bank not to send out monthly statements. She did not want him to know she was trying to save some money, it was not a lot of money, it was there for an emergency. If Clark discovered the bank account, he would demand the money; and Arial, being as stupid as she was would give it all to him.

Arial had reached a point that she could not deal with Clark any longer, she felt like she needed professional help. There was a group of psychologists in town, and Arial was getting desperate, her nerves were shot, she knew she needed to talk to someone. She called and scheduled an appointment; the appointment had to be while Clark was at work, he could never find out, ever! Arial had insurance that covered mental health, but she refused to use it. She was terrified that Clark would discover she was going for therapy. She used the money from her secret savings account, and she always paid with cash, and it was sixty dollars an hour, for Arial that was a lot. At the end of each session, she refused to accept a receipt, she instructed them to place it in her file.

The first session was very eye opening; Arial had to do most of the talking, the doctor took notes. Arial admitted her affair, she admitted everything, and then she went backwards in time. She made it crystal clear that for the first twelve years of her marriage, she was almost a Godly saint. She never disobeyed Clark's orders, she was ridiculed and belittled each day, and she took this mental abuse. She never questioned his authority, if she did he would instruct her very profoundly that she better not push him! Those words and the tone of his voice were enough to repress Arial. She explained to the therapist or at least tried to explain the fear she felt, even if Clark was not home, which he was not most of the time, the fear was always within her. She never knew what to expect when he did arrive home, and she was constantly afraid. The therapist listened very intently as Arial talked. Arial described one incident with difficulty, her third son had gotten very sick at the age of seven and was hospitalized for a lengthy time. Clark blamed her for their son's illness, this devastated Arial. Clark made these remarks in the presence of their son who was very ill at that moment. Because of their son's presence, Arial could not respond, she sat there and stared at Clark, if a stare could have killed Clark, he would have dropped dead that very moment.

The therapist stopped Arial; she opened a drawer and retrieved a paper, the drawing appeared to be a pie with separate slices. Each slice had words typed in them. The therapist placed the paper on the desk in front of Arial, she then proceeded to explain each slice of the pie. She began by referencing Clark with each slice of the paper pie.

The first slice of the pie the therapist pointed at was; USING INTIMIDATIONS; making her afraid by using looks, gestures, destroying her property, and displaying weapons. USING EMOTIONAL ABUSE; putting her down, making her feel bad about herself, calling her names, humiliating her, and making her feel guilty. USING ISOLATION, controlling what she does, what she reads, limiting her outside involvement, and using jealousy to justify actions. MINIMIZING, DENYING BLAME; making light of the emotional abuse, and saying she caused it. USING CHILDREN; making her feel guilty about the children, blaming her for children's sickness, and threatening to take the children away. USING MALE PRIVILEGE; treating her like a servant, making all the decisions, acting like the "master of the castle", and being the one to define men's and women's roles. USING ECONOMIC ABUSE; preventing her from getting or keeping a job, making her ask for money, giving her an allowance, taking her money, and not letting her know and have access to the family income. These actions mentioned were not the complete pie; there are a few more slices. Clark used these particular ones to gain and keep control over Arial.

The therapist said the only reason he had not hit her but once was because she kept quiet, and did as she was told. The therapist insisted that in no way was Arial to begin any defensive actions now. She gave her the number to the women's shelter, and instructed her to call if needed and someone would help her immediately. Arial was not to reveal the number to anyone else.

Arial never had to call the number; she continued her life as she always had.

# Chapter Twenty-Eight

## A Storm was Beginning

Arial sat quietly; waiting, she was going to call again, but she did not have to. The phone finally rang, it was him, it was on the caller ID. She answered quickly, Arial could feel the excitement building, gosh she was so glad she had accidently ran into him, and she told him so. She could hear the excitement in his voice as he talked. They talked about old times and their lives since. Arial still loved this man and she wanted to tell him but she was afraid to, she was so afraid he could not return the sentiment. She would wait, she knew she had to get a better feel of things before she said those words. She knew his number was on the caller ID, and she had never deleted a number, this wonderful man had to explain to Arial how to delete the number. If Clark saw a strange number he would question it. He asked her to call him back, and of course she said she would.

This became a daily call, sometimes more than once, she wanted to see him, and he wanted her to come to his house. Arial was scared, she was concerned about Clark discovering her secret, she also was not certain about this man's true feelings. She did not want to make an ass out of herself, but she did want to see him. There was one more thing she had to consider, her weight, she desperately needed to shed ten pounds. Arial's grown children were also another concern, they were all four married and had children of their own. They loved their dad, but they also knew to a certain degree how their dad was. They did not know everything, because Arial had tried to keep most of it hidden from them. Sometimes now, she wonders if that was a mistake.

Four or five months passed, Arial had been going to his house. She knew she was going to leave Clark, she was not quite sure how or when, but she knew she was leaving. Clark was very difficult to deal with if he thought he had lost any control. Arial knew she would have to leave secretly, it would be a disaster any other way. As it turned out, it was a disaster, more than a disaster; it became a monumental disaster.

Arial went to her mother's house for a couple of weeks, her dad, Frank had died many years before. Eloise, Arial's mother was suspicious, but she kept her thoughts to herself. Arial's four children were disgusted with her, they just about disowned her as their mother. The knowledge that there was another man was more than they could swallow. Arial was adamant, she was not returning to Clark, she did not love him, her children were adults, and they would have to accept this. Those words were easier said than done. Arial was hurt so terribly, she loved her children more than life, and she had given her entire adult life for her children. Arial's oldest son was truly disgusted with her, this she did not expect, in the past he would get so aggravated with his dad, and he would tell Arial that she needed to get out of the house, do something! Arial never would. She was so shocked by her oldest son's looks of almost hate, he went so far as to tell Arial never to call his house again! There was so many things Arial's oldest son did not know about his dad, these things Arial has to this day kept a secret, and she always will.

Arial never gave up on her children. Arial and Clark divorced and Arial married the man she had loved for more than twenty-five years. Slowly, one child at a time, they missed Arial, she was the parent they could always talk to, they could never talk to their dad. They cautiously began to try to understand, Arial oldest son was the last to even try. Deep down in his heart he loved his mother; he knew she had sacrificed a lot to raise them. To this day, twelve years later, he is still recovering, but he does put forth an effort. He likes Arial's new husband, but he does love his dad and that makes it difficult for him. He calls; he and his wife and their kids usually come for special occasions, like Thanksgiving and Christmas. Arial's other three children; they come a lot, her grandchildren spend the night with her, life is almost perfect.

Arial and her second husband live in the country, they are together almost all the time. Each morning they sit on the deck, drink coffee, talk and watch the cows in the pasture. Arial is truly happy, there is no criticism, jealousy, spite work, and he does not try to control her. She paid a huge price for this happiness, but she also paid a huge price for raising her children. She is not sorry for either decision she made, for the first time in her life she did something for herself. In the past, everyone else came first; Arial was always last.

THE END

www.ingramcontent.com/pod-product-compliance
Ingram Content Group UK Ltd.
Pitfield, Milton Keynes, MK11 3LW, UK
UKHW041944190726
13854UKWH00004B/1781

9 781466 976009